MW00785163

Almost Perfect

Disabled Pets and the People Who Love Them

Edited by Mary A. Shafer

Enspirio House
an imprint of Word Forge Books
Ferndale, Pennsylvania
wordforgebooks.com

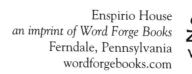

Entire contents of this collection as an anthology copyright © 2008 Enspirio House. Contributors to this anthology hold their individual copyrights. Copying, storage or usage by any means manual or electronic are prohibited without express written consent of the author and publisher. Limited portions of this work may be reproduced for the purpose of review or reportage, as constrained by the Fair Use Act. Unauthorized reproduction in any form, by any person, for any reason will be considered a breach of United States intellectual property laws and a breach of copyright, and will be subject to applicable legal action.

Almost Perfect: Disabled Pets and the People Who Love Them
ISBN 978-0-9771329-2-8
Library of Congress Control Number: 2008905990

PRINTED IN THE U.S.A.

Published by Enspirio House, *an imprint of Word Forge Books*
PO Box 97
Ferndale, PA 18921
Phone 610-847-2456
Fax 610-847-8220
Admin@WordForgeBooks.com
WordForgeBooks.com

Edited by Mary A. Shafer

Cover design by Laura Pritchard
Pritchard Design
Doylestown, PA 18901
Laura@PritchardDesign.com
PritchardDesign.com

Interior design and production by Caryn Newton

Dedication

To all the animals who have ever faced hardship and all the people who have ever loved and cared for them.

Contents

Introduction

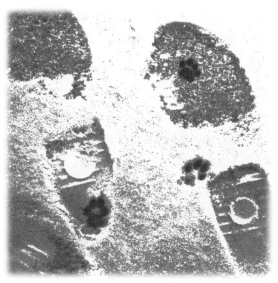

Photo by Susan Bertrand

I first conceived of this book as I sat in my office one day in early October, 2006. It was a beautiful autumn day in south-eastern Pennsylvania, and I looked out on a ridge covered with maples bursting into a riot of seasonal color. I reflected on my good fortune at being able to treat myself to this view each day, changing as it does, but always rewarding. I knew I was lucky to be able to make my living as a writer, doing what I love and bringing people's attention to things that matter.

It was exactly a year since my first book as a self-published author had come out, and it was doing very well. I was living where I'd long wanted to live, in an old stone farmhouse in the rural part of northern Bucks County. I had family nearby, and friends and colleagues even nearer. Best of all, I had a sweet kitty wrapped warmly about my shoulders as I clacked away on my keyboard.

Her name is Idgie, and she had come to us under the most unusual of circumstances. We hadn't been looking for her, and at first, I had even tried to give her away because I feared we wouldn't be able to give her the quality of life she deserved. But the universe conspired to keep her with us, and now I can't imagine my life without her.

The thing is, Idgie was born with no eyes. She's completely blind. People seeing her for the first time always say something like, "Oh, poor thing! How does she get along?" What they don't understand is that Idgie has never, ever seen anything. She has no concept of optical vision. And since you don't miss what you've never had, Idgie doesn't think she's missing anything…and she's not.

She is one of the happiest, most joy-filled creatures I have ever known. And that joy rubs off, every day. When I'm down, she cheers me. When I'm impatient, she reminds me that life is short and nothing is worth getting all worked up about. But mostly, watching her navigate our house with ease, as she makes countless true leaps of faith every day and insists on living in equality alongside our three other sighted cats, humbles me.

Idgie's life makes me realize how rich my world is, how many gifts I've been given, and how deeply I should appreciate it all.

On that October day, this book began to take shape in my mind. I began to think that everyone should be given the opportunity to live with an animal that has disabilities. Because failure to live their lives is not an option, these animals just accept their circumstances and get on with it. No pity parties, no drama. A little frustration sometimes, sure…but overall, they simply keep on keeping on. And they do it with such aplomb that you can't help feeling challenged to do better with what you've been given in your own life.

It occurred to me that it would be worth sharing stories of these amazing creatures, and the positive effect they have on the lives of their families and those around them. I went to the library and the bookstores. I trolled around online, but I didn't find a single volume devoted solely to physically or otherwise challenged pets. So I sent out a call for submissions, and received many excellent pieces.

It was difficult to narrow them down to just the eleven included here, but I think we succeeded in putting together a unique selection that represents the most common domestic pets. We have stories about dogs, cats and even a rat here. And who knows? Maybe there will be more volumes that explore other types of disabled pets. But for now, we hope you find as much inspiration in reading these stories as we have found in living with the animals we wrote about.

I know I speak for all our contributors when I ask you to consider adopting a less-than-perfect pet next time you're thinking about adding an animal companion to your family. Yes, there are challenges to sharing your lives with such critters, but the rewards far outweigh any costs. And it never hurts to make a deposit in the Karma Bank once in a while.

I wish you many tiny tracks crossing your path in this life, and sincerely hope you enjoy *Almost Perfect*.

Mary A. Shafer
Editor
August, 2008

My Tuesdays With Tux
Susan Bertrand

Angels With Paws is a Denver cat shelter where I volunteer. It's here I meet Tux, a beautiful black-and-white "tuxedo" cat.

The first time I see Tux scoot across the shelter floor, I'm surprised at how fast he moves, even on just two legs. I learn that his back legs are paralyzed, and he gets around by using his forelegs to drag his body forward.

At first I am appalled at the horrible unfairness of his physical limitations. Then I grow curious, even fascinated, as I watch him race from one side of the shelter reception room to the other. I notice he leaves a trail of urine. Unfortunately, poor Tux has no control of his bowels—possibly because of a birth defect, or maybe due to the ulcerative tumor on his genital region.

The first time I see him move around, I am so sad. *That poor cat,* I think. *He needs to get outside of his cage and play— smell the scents, swat at the flies, watch the birds and butterflies— enjoy life.* I am determined to work with him, to help him improve—maybe not physically, because there is nothing I can do for him in that regard—but mentally and emotionally. I can maybe improve his outlook on life.

If a human had the ulcerative tumor that Tux has on his rear, he would probably be prescribed a whirlpool bath or hot tub session twice a day. That's what I want to do for Tux, but he'd hate that because it involves water, and…he's a cat.

Tux has warm, expressive eyes, and I find myself wishing he could talk to me. He'd probably tell me that his useless legs aren't really a problem, just a minor inconvenience, especially in the large cage that is his private residence at the shelter.

If I could, I'd arrange for surgery to fix his nerve/muscle problem, if that were possible. I'd be there during the surgery, holding his little paw, stroking his soft fur and feeling the powerful muscles in the front half of his body; waiting for him to wake up, whole again and ready to pounce on life. But that can't be, so instead I talk with the people at Angels with Paws, and suggest a day trip for Tux to my backyard. Jean, the shelter owner, thinks it would be a good idea for him.

Tuesday, 9/13. I pick Tux up from the shelter on Tuesday, my day off, right after lunch. Once his carrier is in the car, he is determined to tell me how unhappy he is about traveling in the car, enclosed in a carrier. The only thing that subdues his yowls is when I stick my fingers into the cage so he can rub his chin on them.

After I stop the car in the garage, Tux stops making noise. The carrier rests on the garage floor for less than a minute, while I open the entrance to our backyard. I want to avoid carrying him through the house, which might stress out Tux and my two cats inside the house. His demeanor changes dramatically once I set the carrier on the grass and open the door.

He immediately crawls out, with big eyes and alert ears. He struggled across a couple feet of patio and onto the freshly mowed grass, stretched out as long as his forelegs will allow, and vigorously kneads the grass. This is one happy kitty. Straining the few inches toward my hands, he rubs them appreciatively with the side of his head. I can read gratitude in those big, intelligent, golden-brown eyes.

Since he has no control of his bladder or bowels, he wee-wee's across the grass. When I pick up his hindquarters by supporting the top of his rear legs, he quickly takes off on his forepaws, leaving a few turds behind. I support his back legs as he races along as quickly as possible. There is just so much to see, hear and smell, and Tux is not planning to waste a single second! I have trouble keeping up with him. Tux and I play "wheelbarrow" until my back can take no more. Tomorrow, my back and butt muscles will ache from supporting his weight as I bend forward.

After the first half-hour of new sights and scents, poor Tux must be experiencing sensory overload, because he heads back toward his carrier in the middle of our small patio for a short respite. He crawls inside, but a minute later his curiosity overrules, and he is back in the grass, eating a few blades and moving eagerly along while swatting at tiny flies and bugs.

This warm Tuesday afternoon, he spends a lot of time resting on the cool grass in the shade of the crabapple tree, his nose in the air, tracking all the exciting new scents.

I try to help him into a special cat "wheelchair," a steel frame with wheels made especially for animals with no use of their back legs. He doesn't like this idea, and fights with me to get back on the grass. The wheeled vehicle is lightweight, but seems too big for him, making his hindquarters rest higher than the front half of his body, and causing him to slide too far forward and out of the support frame.

I need to change the harness so it fits comfortably enough to allow him to pull the wheels along behind him. I'll work on a criss-cross design that will place most of the pressure on his chest and none on his neck. This will stabilize the straps across his chest and front legs to allow him movement, while not being too restrictive.

Queenie, my all-black domestic shorthair, is inside the house, and has seen Tux through the window. I sense she is really interested in checking out this "intruder." After Tux is happily playing on the grass, I quietly let Queenie outside.

She slinks out the door, head low, and creeps low, right over to Tux. He is lying on his side in the grass. I stay very close, in case either of them becomes stressed. Queenie doesn't make a sound, just lays down a short distance away from him and watches as he struggles to move forward in the grass, dragging his lower half. She stares intently at him, not hissing or yowling, no meow or anything.

She seems puzzled. She senses that since I have obviously approved of this intruder onto her private territory, he is probably not a threat, and she would be wise not to cause a fuss.

She slinks off to the far side of the patio, her eye not leaving Tux for a second. A few minutes later she is back, still curious. Tux strains toward her, seeking some introductory scent exchange.

The Queen resents this—*The nerve of him! He's so impertinent!*—and stalks off, then returns to the other side of the patio to keep an eye on him from afar. With a little more time, I believe Queenie will warm up to Tux, and they will become fast friends.

After a couple hours of new sights, sounds and smells, Tux seems to be tiring. He crawls under the corner of the porch overhang to take a nap among some dried leaves. I don't want him overstressed, so I take him back home to the shelter. He promptly falls asleep in his large cage, at least until next week Tuesday. This was all so fun! Tonight he'll dream about chasing bugs and butterflies.

Tuesday, 9/20. I stop in to see Tux and take him on our weekly field trip to my backyard, but he isn't at the shelter. Tux has been at Dr. H.'s veterinary clinic for the past few days, while the doctor checks the progress of his genital area tumor. No real surprise that Tux is at the clinic, because his physical problems are ongoing and not improving. Nobody at the shelter knows how long Tux will be gone. I just hope he'll be back soon.

Tuesday, 9/27. A week later, and Tux is still in the vet clinic. Lisa, another volunteer at the shelter, helps me find the clinic's phone number, and I call there asking to visit Tux.

Shannon, the veterinary technician at the clinic, says that visiting with Tux would be a good idea. I ask about taking Tux on an outing to my backyard, but Dr. H. says that it isn't a good idea for Tux's tumor to come into contact with any bacteria that might be in the grass. I'm disappointed that Tux and I can't continue our Tuesday play dates to my backyard, but I understand the doctor's reasoning, and don't want to aggravate Tux's physical problems.

At three in the afternoon, I leave to visit Tux at the clinic. Shannon directs me to a small exam room in the corner of the office and asks me to wait while she goes to get Tux. She opens the door and sets Tux on the exam table on a clean white towel, then leaves us alone. At first, his front half quivers with excitement or nervousness, but once he recognizes my scent, he starts a purr that lasts the whole hour I'm with him.

He pushes against my hand with his face, inviting me to rub the side of his chin, which I do. I bend my head down over him so that his head is under my chin, and his purr vibrates my throat. He licks my hand, my chin, then my forehead, and chews on a few strands of my hair. I rub his back, stroke his front paws, and gently scratch both sides of his chin using both hands. His useless back legs wobble and quiver with pleasure. He pushes hard against my hands with a strength that belies his disability, in order to increase the contact between us. His pure happiness just overwhelms me, and my tears fall on Tux, his towel, and the little catnip mouse I've brought for him to play with.

He puts his right front paw on my hand and looks into my eyes. His perfectly formed triangular face holds wide, expressive golden-brown eyes. Such a clear, strong gaze doesn't reflect the pain and discomfort he's been feeling; quite the opposite. He seems pleased by the attention and affection he's receiving and excited to be in a different environment. When his catnip mouse falls to the floor, he pushes forward with his front paws and tries to jump off the exam table to retrieve it, but I held onto him. He is saying, "I wanna get that mouse. I can do it— C'mon, let me go!"

A little later, when I pull over a chair and put my arm on top of the table where he sits, he turns to his left and rests both front legs on my arm, still purring. The white towel under Tux starts showing signs of urine spots. There are also small, dark flecks of dried blood and feces, and a few smears of fresh blood.

After a while, Tux seems to be getting tired and his eyes begin to close, so I call Shannon to take him back to his cage so he can sleep. I speak with her for a few minutes, trying to understand Tux's physical condition and future options.

She tells me Tux was found nearby several months ago, crawling across the street on his two front legs. Those who found him assumed he'd been hit by a car. Someone brought him to the vet clinic nearby, and Shannon had named him Tux. When Dr. H. found out that Tux had nerve and spinal damage that couldn't be repaired, he called the Angels With Paws shelter. The shelter has housed him for a couple months, hoping to find a permanent home for him.

It has been very difficult for the shelter to find an adoptive parent with the time, resources, knowledge and energy to care for Tux. He will need special accommodations, since he leaves a trail of urine wherever he crawls. He also needs medical care and a lot more special treatment and time than most cats do. So far, no one has volunteered to take on the added responsibilities of this special-needs cat.

Shelter volunteers have arranged chiropractic and acupuncture treatments for Tux's affliction, but neither seems to have helped much. The doctor seems to think that Tux's medical condition or quality of life will not improve. Even if his genital tumor is removed, he will never regain use of his back legs, nor have bowel or urine control.

By talking with Shannon, the vet tech, I find out that not only is Tux in pain, but the large tumor on his genital region is necrotic. This means that the tissue there is no longer living and healthy. Shannon tells me that she and Dr. H. were cleaning Tux's genital area earlier Tuesday morning and the prepuce—the foreskin of his penis—dropped off. She says dead tissue has been flaking off his tumor for weeks, and the tumor may be cancerous.

Dr. H. now believes that the best thing for Tux would be euthanasia. Jean, the shelter owner, is opposed to euthanasia, and doesn't want Tux put to sleep. I ask Shannon how she feels about it, and she and I agree that sleep would be better for Tux than a life of pain in a small cage for the rest of his life. Cats can live for twenty years or more, and to think that poor Tux would spend the next twenty years or so in his painful, deteriorating condition is very sad.

Shannon agrees with my suggestion that I call Jean and talk with her about Tux. It will be very difficult for me, but I will make the call. If the decision is finally made to euthanize, I want to be there with Tux when he goes.

A couple days later, I hear that Jean has agreed with Dr. H. that the best thing for Tux would be permanent sleep. I am relieved that I don't have to call Jean to discuss euthanasia, but

I am also very sad, because I'll miss Tux terribly. He'll never again feel the grass beneath his paws, never chase a bug, never argue with the magpies on the back fence; but neither will he feel discomfort. He'll be free from infection and pain, and free from his cage forever.

No matter what happens with Tux, I will always remember meeting that powerful, expressive gaze that said to me, "Don't worry, everything will be all right."

Thursday, 9/29. The call is waiting for me when I get home from work Thursday night. The red light on the answering machine flashes angrily, and I dread taking the message.

"This is Shannon from Dr. H.'s vet clinic. I'm calling to let you know that Tux's euthanasia is scheduled for Friday morning at ten. If you'd like to come in this afternoon to see Tux, we'll be very busy here, but I'm certain we can find a place for you to visit with him if you want to. Please call the clinic."

I feel my stomach clench and my eyes start to fill. It is too late; the clinic is already closed for the day. Will I be able to see Tux tomorrow? I'll call in the morning. My boss will need to grant me a free hour on Friday. I want to be there with Tux on his last day.

Friday, 9/30. I arrange to take an hour off work, and leave at nine-thirty a.m. on Friday. I pull up to the vet clinic fifteen minutes later, get out of the car and hear, "Hey."

Penny and Tina, two other volunteers at the Angels With Paws shelter, have driven into the parking lot of the vet clinic at the same time I have. I'm surprised but pleased to see them, because this means that Tux will spend his last minutes getting love and attention from all three of us. We walk into the clinic together. Nobody says anything.

Sean, the vet tech, ushers us into the same room in which I visited Tux three days earlier. He says the doctor will be delayed for a few minutes, because he is in the middle of a neuter surgery. Sean brings Tux in and sets him on a soft, blue fleece blanket.

All three of us surround Tux on the three sides of the small exam table. We shower him with love, petting, rubbing and stroking his small broken body, and mumbling sweet things into his ears. When he leans to one side, I am able to see the tumor in his genital region. It appears to glow green and yellow with infection and pus, and it looks terribly painful.

Tina, Penny and I talk about how Tux reminds us of specific characteristics of our own family cats. Tina's Baby is just as inquisitive; Penny's Jojo has just as much energy and, like Tux, is sometimes a little troublemaker. My Queenie has the same direct, intelligent gaze. Penny has heard that the doctor gave Tux pain medication earlier, and Tina and I nod in gratitude. Despite the medication, Tux seems as active and energetic as usual.

Dr. H. steps in the door and says, "Well, it's almost time. Are we ready? Has everybody been through this before?" He looks at each one of us.

Only Penny nods, so the doctor patiently explains to Tina and me what we might expect.

"The drug is actually an overdose of anesthetic used for surgery," explains the doctor. "First the respiratory system relaxes and breathing stops, then the heart. In regard to the breathing, sometimes you'll hear a gasp, or something that sounds like a gasp, caused by the large diaphragm muscle contracting. Then there may be urination or defecation, though that doesn't always happen.

"We've got just a few things left to prepare. It'll be just a few more minutes." Then the doctor retreats through the door.

All three of us don't have much to say. We murmur a few words in turn, just to reassure each other about how Tux will soon be free from pain. Then we simply stand without speaking, each with a hand on Tux, and each outdoing the other in our brave attempts not to cry.

Tux purrs up a storm, but doesn't make any other sounds. He is surely aware of all the love in this little room, directed toward him.

Tina has brought a throwaway camera, and gets a few good pictures of Tux in the morning light from the large window in the exam room. I take a picture of Tina with Tux clasped to her neck. He appears to be clothed in her long, blond hair. She gets a shot of Tux licking my forehead. She also snaps a good one of Tux excitedly looking out the window at something he desperately wants to chase.

Tina tells Tux how his legs will soon be whole and he'll be chasing those butterflies. She says, "You're almost home, sweetheart. Those front legs are already climbing the stairs (to the Rainbow Bridge)."

A few minutes later, the doctor returns with a small syringe, half-filled with bright pink fluid. I stand at the left side of the table facing Tux, but I happen to be in the way of the doctor. Just as I move to the front of the table, Sean, the vet tech, comes in to assist. All five of us are crowded into this small exam room.

Penny, who has had experience holding a cat to prepare for injection, holds Tux's left back leg firmly, as the rest of us help keep Tux in position on his left side. He looks surprised and a little scared, but he doesn't move at all.

Tina has Tux's head between her hands, and Sean helps hold down Tux's body, so the injection can be made safely. The only part of Tux available for me to touch is his forehead. I use two fingers to stroke the small area between his ears, and feel a great sadness.

Dr. H. spreads the hairs on the inside of Tux's left thigh to find a vein. He inserts the needle and a tiny drop of blood appears. As the pink fluid in the syringe slowly enters his bloodstream, Tux's eyes visibly relax a bit, then a little more. Tina is talking to him and holding her head close to his. Penny is concentrating hard on holding Tux still during the injection, and trying to avoid any emotional reaction. She's like that.

"Tux, baby," says Tina, "it's all right. You'll be okay, sweetheart. Don't worry. We love you so much."

Dr. H. speaks to the vet tech. "Sean, I don't know if he's had enough. This vein isn't working very well. Let's try the other leg. I'd like to try to get a little more into him, just to make sure."

Since the room is too small to include all five of us at the table, I stand back and give those who are more experienced room to work with Tux. I watch all four of them gently turn Tux to his right side. Now he's looking directly at me with his half-closed eyes.

Sean backs up a bit and wraps his hand over Tux's back leg, covering his tumor and stabilizing the injection area with his gloved hands. Tina's hands move from Tux's head to his back. I am able to squeeze in and cradle Tux's sleepy head in my left hand, and with my right, I softly rub his chin. His eyes don't close, but they stop darting around, the inner cat eyelid moving toward the center of the pupil. Gradually, he begins to just stare, unseeing. Now he is finally at peace and free from pain.

The doctor says, "I guess that's it," but I continue to stroke Tux's head and gently scratch his chin. Tina's hand moves down Tux's back. We just don't want to leave him. We don't want him to be gone. A heavy sadness settles in the room.

Penny quietly talks to Dr. H. about taking Tux's body back to the shelter, but the doctor says he will take care of it. I thank the doctor for allowing me to be present, knowing Tux's body will be cared for respectfully. I say goodbye to Penny and Tina, then turn and walk out of the clinic.

I get into my car, but my throat hurts and I find myself taking deep breaths, trying not to choke up. I have to get back to work.

As I drive, I think about Tux's clear, strong gaze assuring me that things will be okay, and I wonder what I am going to do without him. I miss him already.

The author's favorite picture of Tux. "It truly shows his fascination with everything. Period," she says. "He has a perpetually surprised look on his face…that's because he's perpetually surprised. I think all the pictures I have of him show the same expression."

About the Author

A native of Hartford, Wisconsin, Susan Bertrand now lives at the foothills of the majestic Rocky Mountains in Arvada, Colorado. She and her husband Kim are avid skiers and take full advantage of their convenient location. When not on the slopes, Sue makes her living as a medical assistant and medical records reviewer.

In her spare time, Sue volunteers with the Angles With Paws cat shelter, where she's helped homeless felines since 2003. She manages their thrift store, all proceeds of which go to support the shelter. Sue also participates in the shelter's Adopt-A-Thons, Pet Pictures with Santa, yard sales and other fund-raising events.

Susan Bertrand is on the right, holding Roxy, a black-and-white "magpie," whom Sue says "is very vocal and needs a lot of attention." Sue's husband Kim is at left, holding Queenie, whom, according to Sue, lives up to her name in demanding regal treatment. They all live happily in Arvada, Colorado.

Love Is Blind: Colbi
Joyce Grant-Smith

Lots of people fall in love over the Internet. It has become such a common occurrence, I suppose I shouldn't have been surprised when I succumbed.

I gazed at his photo attachment on my e-mail. He had dark, pleading eyes and a sweet face, and my heart melted. The funny wrinkle to all this was that the e-mail was from a representative from the Nova Scotia SPCA and the photo was of a six-month-old, husky-shepherd pup. He had been rescued from a horrendous puppy mill situation and was in need of a home.

I'm a soft touch, ask anybody. My houseful of cats and dogs is testimony to that fact. So when the pup's sad face filled my computer screen, I was a goner. I began the paperwork that would allow me to bring him home.

It took several weeks before all the red tape was sorted out, but at last, I was told that I could collect the young dog from the SPCA shelter in Dartmouth, Nova Scotia.

Evidently, not all the red tape had been successfully clipped and tucked away, however. After driving two hours to reach the Dartmouth shelter, I learned that, through some communication foul-up, the pup had been moved to another location. He was now an hour and a half farther away.

I could have just turned and gone home, or I could have chosen one of the other gorgeous purebred huskies kenneled right there at the Dartmouth SPCA, awaiting a home. But I didn't. The image of that sweet face would have haunted me for the rest of my life. I made arrangements to meet the SPCA worker with the pup in Truro, climbed back in my car, and drove on.

Finally, the rendezvous had been successfully orchestrated. The Society worker gratefully handed over the very frightened pup with a few quick words, something about him being "visually impaired" and "gulping water—maybe diabetic." I placed the pup on the car seat beside me, where he cowered on the proffered blanket. The Society worker drove off, and I was left with my new companion.

The enormity of what I had just taken on suddenly hit me. Any sane person would have made a beeline to the SPCA shelter, done some major backpedaling, and left the pup in their care. Here was a young dog, still woefully thin and bedraggled even after a month of SPCA care. He had special, perhaps very costly, health issues. His vision was "impaired," to what extent I was not yet sure. In his brief six months on this earth, he had never been handled, never had any form of training (house-breaking or any other kind), had never even been inside a house. It sounded like a recipe for utter disaster, and it should have been.

Miraculously, it did not work out that way.

The pup hardly moved a muscle during the whole drive home. I'd had visions of him thrashing in total panic due to the movement of the car. Instead, he flattened himself to the seat, occasionally lifting his head and sniffing the air.

Once we arrived at the house, I led him inside. He was obviously not used to being touched or to having a collar and leash, so he tugged nervously. He didn't panic or become aggressive, though.

He met our other four dogs. They accepted this new arrival as a natural course of events. He seemed cheered to realize there were other dogs around. This, at least, was something he understood.

The first evening was a bit rough on the pup. Because my husband and I didn't know the extent of his "visual impairment," it took a while to realize that he couldn't see the furniture to avoid bumping into it. He didn't understand stairs, because he'd never experienced them before and he couldn't see those, either. At last, we had to admit that his impairment was complete. He was totally blind.

We blocked the stairs of our split-level home, preventing him from tumbling up or down, and we helped him sort out where the furniture was. He hated being restrained by the leash, so eventually we let him loose to explore the main floor of the house unrestricted.

One reason he didn't completely panic in this strange new situation was our alpha dog, Casey. A husky-lab cross, Casey has always been the peacemaker. He's the fellow who always steps between any squabbling members of the household (cat, dog or human) to restore order. He also tends to be the greeter, meeting new arrivals and showing them the ropes.

Casey sized the new fellow up and decided that he needed some help. He took it upon himself to lead the pup around the house. Then, when we went outside to begin house training, Casey positioned the pup at his shoulder and led him around the yard. It wasn't long before I was able to let the pup off the dreaded leash because I knew he would stay glued to Casey's flank.

We tried to close the pup in our small galley kitchen that first night, thinking the small space would discourage him from moving around and hurting himself. Bad idea. He found the confinement terrifying. He thrashed around and desperately tried to jump out over the barrier we had set up. Maybe it was too much like the hell he had endured for so long at the puppy mill. After trying to calm him for several minutes and realizing that he wasn't going to be content in an enclosed space, we just let him have the freedom of the main floor. He paced around a bit, bouncing off the furniture like a slow pinball, then found a quiet corner and curled up to sleep.

We finally turned in for the night and tried to get some sleep, too. The pup visited me in my dreams. He stood before me, his sweet masked face focused on mine. He spoke to me, saying, "My name is Colbi."

I woke up, wondering where that name came from. I hadn't remembered ever hearing it before. When I went downstairs in the morning, I called to the pup.

"Come here, Colbi."

Though the pup had never been taught to respond to any form of command, he came right to me. So Colbi he was, and he has happily answered to that name ever since.

Not everything went as smoothly as learning Colbi's name. House training took a lot of time and patience. It wasn't that Colbi was uncooperative. The training was just a completely new concept to him.

It didn't help that he gulped every drop of water that was placed in his dish as soon as it was set on the floor. He had been so deprived of food and water that, when he had it available to him, he felt he had to get as much as he could, as fast as he could. He feared he might never have it again. We had to ration his water, giving him a little bit many times through the day, so he wouldn't gorge himself and become sick. It took months before we could leave a full water dish on the floor and not have him immediately drain it.

We worried that the heavy water consumption might signal that he was diabetic, but our vet tested him and was able to assure us that he did not have that issue. His previous deprivation may have caused his kidneys to be weakened somewhat, though. We've had to adapt to this, making sure he gets outside at least once during the night, as he can't make it eight hours without relieving himself. Since my middle-aged bladder also finds it difficult to make it through the night without a bathroom break, this doesn't present as big problem as one might think!

Despite all his mistreatment, Colbi's personality is amazingly kind and gentle. Initially, he did become fearful when put in new situations, such as going to the vet. After all, he couldn't see what was happening or where he was, but it never occurred to him to snap or growl. At such times, I learned to keep him securely against my leg in an exaggerated "heel" position. He placed his trust in me, letting me lead him into the unknown.

He has always liked to be close to me, following me around the farm and lying under the kitchen table when I have my meals. It took a while for him to learn to enjoy being touched, though. Not having been handled as a pup, he was puzzled by people stroking him. Because he couldn't see a hand coming toward him, such touches would often startle him. To counter this, I learned to speak to him first, then reach out to touch him.

It took nearly a year, but finally Colbi got so that he sought attention and would cuddle up against me, asking to be stroked. Now he'll tuck his head under my elbow, asking me to caress his ears. When I do this, he closes his eyes blissfully, basking in the affection.

Colbi grew to become a very handsome dog. He wears the black husky facemask. His outer coat is black with tan accents, with a lovely dove-gray undercoat as thick and downy as rabbit fur. He is our gentle giant, tipping the scales at close to one hundred pounds.

Colbi gradually learned the layout of the farm well enough that he no longer needed to be Casey's shadow. He struck out on his own, using the feel of the terrain under his feet, the smells, and the sounds around him to navigate. He knew where it was open and safe to run and he galloped along, bounding joyfully like any other dog.

That's not to say he never had an accident. He received

the occasional scrape or bruise from bumping into things like clothesline poles or parked cars. At these times, he would give his head a shake, take a breath and carry on. He accepted these incidents as part of life.

One summer day, he was running along the driveway from the barn to the house. This was a space that he felt was safe for a really good romp. The gravel under his feet let him know there was nearly two hundred feet of clear, level running room. However, on this afternoon, my rotund old collie, Breezey, was standing on the driveway, waiting for me. She wasn't moving, so Colbi didn't hear her. He broadsided her, his hundred pounds bowling her over as he ran full-tilt. Breezey rolled like an overturned barrel for several feet. Colbi barely hesitated in his stride, hardly aware of the collision, and carried on.

I rushed over to Breezey as she hauled herself to her feet. She wasn't injured, except for her pride. When Colbi returned to see what I was doing, Breezey let him know in no uncertain terms, with growls and gnashing teeth, that she was highly insulted by his behavior. Poor fellow, I'm sure he was very apologetic.

The first winter posed a problem for Colbi. When the snow came and drifted in great piles, his familiar landscape suddenly changed. He struggled with this for a day or so, then applied strategies that had worked for him before. He became Casey's shadow till he figured out the new paths through the snow. His resourcefulness was inspiring.

Colbi taught us quite a lot about how to aid the visually impaired. Talking about what we are about to do before doing it prevents scaring or confusing him. He has learned to slow down and check out the area if we warn him with "wait" or "careful."

Furniture rarely gets moved at our house. It's a good thing I don't have any burning impulses to experiment with home décor. We also have to keep things neat around the place. Clutter on the counters or tables is okay, but we don't leave stuff on the floor that the dog might stumble over.

The cars are always parked in the same place in the driveway, and bikes have to stay in the garage when not in use. These little things keep Colbi safe and feeling confident as he moves about his world.

When Colbi was about three years old, we adopted another pup, Calleen. She was a border collie mix, full of mischief and energy. Calleen brought out the puppy in Colbi. We hadn't seen him play too much before, since our other dogs were older and fairly sedate. They weren't much for toys anymore. Once Calleen came on the scene, we invested in balls and chew toys to help keep her amused and out of trouble.

Colbi was thrilled to have a playmate. They tore around the yard after one another, Colbi using his ears to track Calleen's presence. The day she realized that if she wasn't moving, Colbi couldn't find her, you could almost hear her "Aha!" She has made the chase game far more challenging for him since then!

Colbi now had chew toys to gnaw. He had balls to run after. He listened for the ball hitting the ground, finding it by the bounces. It had never occurred to me to try this with him until he joined in Calleen's games. I felt a bit guilty for limiting his experiences because of my perceptions of what he could do.

Colbi doesn't realize that he's disabled. He only perceives possibilities, not limitations. He figures life is pretty darned good. He has other dog friends. He gets plenty of food and water, a warm place to sleep, and toys to play with. He has a family that loves and accepts him for just who he is.

What we have received in return is complete trust, companionship and affection. Colbi has broadened my mind, letting me see new, wonderful possibilities. I feel humbled by the depth of wisdom and acceptance he possesses.

When people ask me why I took on so difficult a "project" as a blind, untrained dog, I smile and say that Colbi is a miracle who has bestowed more blessings upon me than I will ever give him.

Colbi stands in the yard where he learned to love romping.

About the Author

Author Joyce Grant-Smith lives with her husband, Les, their two children Jesse and Alexis, and numerous dogs, cats, and horses, in the beautiful Annapolis Valley in Nova Scotia, Canada. A sixth-grade teacher, Joyce volunteers at the TLC Animal Shelter in Digby, N.S. She has also volunteered for many years at Mandala Riding and Awareness  Center in Hampton, which offers therapeutic riding classes.

In 2003, Joyce was awarded the Joyce Barkhouse Award for Children's Writing. The following year, her book, *The Latch*, was published by Bruncreek Books. She had two stories, *Dog Tales from the Soul* and *Happy Endings, Volumes I and II* published in two anthologies by K&B Products the next year. Then, in 2006, Joyce was nominated for the Hackmatack Children's Choice Award. And in 2007, her piece, *Teacher's Miracles*, was published by Adams Media.

Love Conquers All: Grover
Linda Bruno

We watched, our hearts breaking, as the sweet little kitten flipped heels-over-head right into his water dish. It wasn't the first time. Since we had taken him in as a foster cat ten days earlier, we had witnessed this scene over and over again. It was as if his little back legs were connected to hydraulic lifts that wouldn't stop in time and—*whoops!*—up and over he went, a howl of frustration expressed with every tumble.

When he wasn't suffering from this cruel joke of nature, he was struggling to stand and walk. The catchphrase from a toy company that "Weebles wobble but they don't fall down™," often came to mind as we watched his determined efforts. He obviously wasn't a Weeble. Falling down was a fact of life for him. Add to all of this the periodic seizures he suffered, and it was hard to disagree with our local Humane Society volunteer that we should "wait a couple of weeks to see if he gets better…"

She had called late one evening, asking if we could find room in our home—and our hearts—to foster an injured kitten that had been found on a city street. Our own animal "inventory" was at its limit with three cats and a dog, but mention "kitten" and "injured" in the same sentence, and there is no discussion.

"Bring him over." We would foster him until we could find his forever home.

Laura, the volunteer, arrived carrying a smelly, yowling creature inside a normal cat carrier…but there was nothing normal about its contents.

Even at just a few weeks old, the kitten's deep golden eyes were riveting. It was hard to tell what color he was, as his fear had caused him to lose all control and he was covered in his own mess.

Laura lifted him from the carrier, saying, "Looks like we'd better give him a bath."

As she held him under the warm water, gently rubbing shampoo into his dirty, matted fur, we slowly recognized a beautiful white-and-tiger pattern emerging on his coat. As he squirmed and mewed, Laura told us the story of Grover, so-named because he had been found on Grove Street, and her two little boys loved Sesame Street—a natural fit.

She explained that she had received a call about a kitten that couldn't walk. As she arrived at the scene, she noticed that although his front legs moved normally, his back legs simply weren't working right.

"He may have been hit by a car," she told us matter-of-factly.

That's when we were given the two-week timeline as to when a decision would need to be made about his future. Her comment about waiting a couple weeks to see if he gets better hung in the air. We could fill in the blanks. Our Humane Society was an all-volunteer organization, supported solely by donations. It simply wasn't realistic to consider keeping a cat that would require an inordinate amount of care—and an inordinate amount of the too-scarce funding available.

Ten days later, we had witnessed none of the improvement we had hoped for. What we had witnessed, though, was a touching show of fierce independence, determination and courage from this little furball.

As fate would have it, the two-week deadline drawing near, I received a newsletter from Best Friends Animal Society in Kanab, Utah. The newsletter of this sanctuary for abused and abandoned animals featured an entire page dedicated to the special cathouse—a home for cats that couldn't walk. I immediately e-mailed the sanctuary about Grover's symptoms. Within hours, I had my answer. It sounded as if Grover suffered from cerebellar hypoplasia (CH), a condition that can result from the mama cat contracting distemper while pregnant.

To make sure we had diagnosed him correctly, we drove nearly two hours to the veterinary school at Ohio State University. Grover sat contentedly on my lap the entire trip, not knowing where he was going, but trusting that since we were taking him, it had to be okay.

There, Grover was given a complete exam along with his very first nickname—Pud-Pud—by the young female student who had fallen in love with him at first sight. Pud-Pud was an obviously shortened form of Puddin'—likely a reference to his sweet personality. The CH diagnosis was confirmed as was a mild heart murmur, but we were assured that with proper care, Grover could live a somewhat normal life.

Excited to know that he didn't have to be put to sleep because of his disability, we were nevertheless saddened to realize it was time to find him his forever home. When we got home, we put the word out and set a date to make sure we kept the goal in sight: Find a home for Grover, the kind of home this special little guy deserved.

In the meantime, the term "high-maintenance" took on new meaning as we custom-designed a litter box he could use on his own, and cleaned up the occasional mess when he didn't quite make it. Hour after hour was spent bubble-wrapping the sharp edges protruding from furniture, fixtures and fireplace hearths, to protect him from uncontrolled contact.

We placed a chair in front of the picture window so Grover could watch the squirrels scampering across the front yard. A perfectly good towel was sacrificed to cover the chair, so he could raise and lower himself when he got bored with the view.

A special front-page article in our local newspaper chronicled the budding friendship between Grover, the handicapped cat, and Abby, our 55-pound Australian shepherd mix dog. Abby merely tolerated Grover's constant attention, but Grover had found his new best friend. Readers of the paper learned that animals are not disposable just because they have a handicap.

We slowly discovered that this little guy had quite a vocabulary. It took weeks for us to figure out that his nine-thirty p.m. chattering was his attempt to get us to leave the computer and have some snuggle time. Once he was happy with the amount of snuggling he'd had, he told us in no uncertain terms that it was his bedtime, and since he had his own room, it was time for us to put him to bed. If we left his door open thinking he might not be quite ready to go to sleep, he would often struggle back to wherever we were and let us know that bedtime means a dark room and a closed door! Obediently, we would take him in our arms, put him in bed, turn off the light and close the door. He would sleep peacefully until our alarm clock went off the next morning.

The days ticked by as the time drew near when Grover would leave his loving foster home. We had learned so much from him: Persistence, as he made his way very carefully to the water dish when he was thirsty and there was no one to help him. Trust, as we scooped him up time after time to carry him where we thought he wanted to go. Courage, as he played with Abby, nearly ten times his size. And dignity, as he made his way from room to room the best he could, ignoring the looks of pity from visitors to our home.

Many were obviously thinking—and some had the nerve to say it—"Why don't you just put him to sleep?"

As I think back to the day he was finally adopted, I remember the questions that were never far from our minds. Would anybody love him the way we did? Would they take the time to help him in and out of his litter box when he voiced a cry for help? Would they even take the time to learn his special vocabulary, so they could tell the difference between his needing the litter box and being hungry? Would someone be willing to bubble-wrap the sharp edges of his life?

Maybe. Maybe not. And yet, Grover did find his forever home.

As I watch him sleeping in the sunshine, I realize it's been more than five years since Grover became a permanent part of our lives.

High-maintenance? Yes, I suppose some would say that. Hard work? Yeah, that too. Some say he was lucky we took him in as a foster cat, but we are the lucky ones. Every day, we are thankful that life brought us Grover. And every day, he teaches us so much.

The most important lesson? Love really does conquer all.

Even as a kitten, Grover exhibited signs of cerebellar hypoplasia, a disorder found in cats and dogs in which part of the brain is not fully developed at birth. The symptoms include jerky movements, tremors and generally uncoordinated motion. Afflicted animals often fall down and have difficulty walking.

About the Author

Author Linda Bruno, now of Ocala, Florida, provided foster homes for seventeen cats in two years during her volunteer time at her local humane society in Ohio.

She currently makes her living as a writer and workshop facilitator. Her first published work was a piece for *Chicken Soup for the Cat Lover's Soul*, published by Health Communications in 2005. That was followed in 2006 with one of her stories being included in *Letters to my Teacher*, published by Adams Media. The following year, Adams again tapped Linda to provide a story for their title *Letters to My Mother*. This fall, yet another of Linda's stories is to be published in Adams' *A Cup of Comfort: Christmas Through a Child's Eye*.

An Unlikely Hero: Simon
Carol Downie

Simon, a three-legged barn cat with about as many teeth, had an indomitable spirit and an unquenchable purr.

I first met Simon at the barn where my younger daughter stabled her horse. Simon hip-hopped fearlessly among the horses; his spotless, fuzzy white fur glowed eerily against the dirt floor and dusty gloom of the barn. He balanced his hindquarters on a single leg to propel himself along and headed confidently toward our feet. His leg had been amputated above the hip some years previous, either due to a mishap or a tangle with another animal. The same incident was responsible for his tattered ears and missing teeth. As barn cats go, Simon had been well-cared for by his original owner. He had been neutered, his injured leg had been surgically amputated and, as we found out later, his vaccinations had been kept up-to-date until about two years previous, when the barn changed owners.

Simon was a favorite among the girls who boarded their horses at his barn. His friendly nature and crooked "smile" charmed the girls into swooping him up for a snuggle inside their down jackets while they went about their barn chores in the frigid Minnesota cold. His pink ears and nose and one pink-padded front paw protruded from the jacket front. He blinked contentedly and emitted a rumbling purr.

Mothers' Day arrived and, shortly thereafter, my daughter dropped by with Simon cradled in her arms. One of his three remaining legs had been broken when he got caught napping under the tractor mower. The new owner didn't want to be bothered with the cat; my daughter quickly had talked the owner into giving Simon to her—meaning, to me—for mending. And so, Simon became another of our rescued creatures, joining a long parade of flying squirrels, woodchucks, dogs, cats, goslings, pigeons, raccoons, 'possums and bunnies. We nurtured them until they could safely return to the wild, or they lived out their lives with us—sometimes a few minutes until they died in our hands, assured only of a violence-free death, or a decade or two, as was the case with the dogs and cats.

Simon purred sonorously as he rested in my daughter's arms. She returned to work; I took Simon to the vet. During the examination, Simon remained docile and continued to purr so loudly and persistently that even the doctor was impressed and took Simon around to the other technicians in wonder. The leg was totally dislocated but not broken; resetting it would cost upwards of $600. I reminded myself that this was as much about my daughter as about the cat.

"Well, if we're going to do this," I said, "I suppose we should have him tested first—worms, ear mites, blood work for the anesthesia, and, of course, feline leukemia." Parasites: negative. Ear mites: negative. Blood profile: "down the middle" normal. Feline leukemia: positive. Tears burned my eyes.

Feline leukemia (FeLV), a fatal viral disease, threatens the lives of thousands of domestic and wild cats each year. No cure and no palliative pharmaceutical therapy are available. Historically, the disease has been considered so highly contagious among cats that those with a positive test result were destroyed automatically, cats, kittens, family pets or feral, no matter. Among those cats that are not euthanized, 83% die within three years of diagnosis and 50% within a year.

I called my daughter. "I'd like you to be here when we put him down. We don't have much choice." She arrived with a sheaf of papers in her hand, Internet-gleaned information about FeLV that augmented what the vet had given me. The doctor showed us into an empty exam room to let us cry in private while we sorted through what we were finding out. Feline leukemia has not been found to be contagious to other species, including dogs and humans. It is highly contagious to cats and is transmitted through body fluid exposure: mutual grooming, bite wounds and, less often, shared water dishes and litter boxes. The disease itself can be debilitating but also interferes with the cat's ability to ward off other diseases and infections. Trauma can activate latent feline leukemia.

Though he tested positive on the ELISA test initially, and later was confirmed infected, Simon was asymptomatic—and such a nice cat. I searched for reasons not to have him put down. I had an older, 75-pound black Lab, but no other cats. I lived on a large property where he could do some supervised roaming to satisfy his "outdoor cat" lifestyle without endangering other animals. I crumbled and made a deal with Simon: I'd keep him going as long as I reasonably could but would take no extreme measures to combat the leukemia should he begin exhibiting symptoms. The vet raised his eyebrows but agreed that my decision was a safe—and humane—alternative. However, I should not expect Simon to live long, given the statistics.

Since it was so close to Mothers' Day and we knew approximately how old Simon was, we declared his birth date to be Mothers' Day 1990, making him at least 11 years old when he ceased being a barn cat and became a lap child.

A week later, I hosted my oldest daughter's wedding in my gardens. The guests remarked on the lovely wedding service, the lush and colorful setting—and Simon, hippity-hopping along on two legs and a cast, with a silly "smile" on his face.

Simon hadn't been in the family long enough for him and the dog to accept each other when a huge thunderstorm struck during the night. The old black lab was afraid of thunder and so, apparently, was Simon. I awoke to find both the dog and the cat scrambling into bed with me, neither of which was allowed to sleep there. I spent the night with my arm hanging over the edge of the bed, holding down the two animals and patting them as they lay cowering underneath. After the storm, they had settled whatever differences they had and remained comfortably good friends thereafter.

Simon used up 13 or 14 of his "nine lives" with us. His tail was gashed open when the wind slammed a door shut on it. He would sneak in under the dog's chin while she was eating and steal her supper; the one thing that would trigger a growl from the dog. Simon broke an arthritic joint in his leg when the old dog tripped over him and fell on top of the cat. Simon would occasionally disappear overnight if his jaunts took him too far astray to get home before dark. He got locked into an unheated construction site for 11 days in the middle of the winter, sending me into sheer panic. When he came home, he was two pounds lighter and "swearing" a blue streak, but otherwise unharmed.

Come spring, I found him sunning himself in the same spot where I had seen a little red fox the day before. And, periodically, he cast all caution to the wind and confronted stray cats, vociferously but bloodlessly, when they intruded on his territory. These victims included one four-week-old kitten that came caterwauling out of the woods and onto the front porch.

Every injury meant another trip to the vet and, while Simon protested during the ride, he never showed any aggression or ill temper toward me or any of his caregivers. His purr became legendary. Every trauma he encountered raised my anxiety titer: was this going to be the event that tipped him over the edge and into active, symptomatic, fatal feline leukemia?

Simon was a working cat and did his best to keep a healthy check on the chipmunk, rabbit, and mouse populations. He tried to keep the old dog company, or, more likely, was stealing her bed. Simon would edge in next to the dog on her overstuffed cushion; a really touching sight, big black dog, small white cat, side by side. Simon occasionally groomed the dog's shoulder with his little pink tongue; the dog responded with a slurpy lick that almost sent Simon sprawling. Oddly enough, the dog was intimidated by the cat, actually by any cat, and would give up her bed as soon as Simon was comfortably settled in.

Simon's most important job, however, was keeping me company. I was newly retired, my adult children had homes of their own and my husband worked long hours. Simon needed me. My husband could tell where I was by where he found the animals. If more than a couple of hours had passed since I had petted Simon, he would sit down at my feet, look directly into my face and meow plaintively. He would continue until I picked him up and he had received what he considered to be his due allotment of affection. He enjoyed being carried upright, braced against my hip like a small child, and would put his "arms" around my neck. Evenings were our special time together. As my husband and I relaxed in the library, Simon would saunter past my husband and approach my chair. He then spent as much of the evening as I would give him curled up in my lap, which, I might add, seems precariously close to my heart.

I began caring for my infant granddaughter and worried that Simon would become jealous and naughty or aggressive. However, he simply adopted the baby as another source of affection and seemed to thrive on having his whiskers pulled and his ears pinched. He returned the attention by giving her a gentle pat, pat, pat with his claws retracted. The baby soon learned to be gentle, too, and to pat Simon and smooth his unruly white fur with soft strokes and an open hand. When the granddaughter's baby sister was born, the older child was dismayed and shoved away the newborn in protest. Her father rebuked her quietly in language she immediately understood. "No,

Naomi. Be gentle. Pat the baby, just like you pat Simon."

The old dog eventually died and left Simon without other animal companionship. Simon was approaching 17 years of age and had been asymptomatic for over six years, perhaps as long as eight or nine, based on his vaccination history. But as the months passed and Simon began losing weight, I wondered about the leukemia. I re-examined a spot on his hip that we had thought was a scar and a biopsy of which had been negative three years earlier. A new biopsy came back positive with a diagnosis of mast cell carcinoma.

By Valentine's Day, I knew the end was near and feared I had already waited longer than was kind. I couldn't bear to have him euthanized on Valentine's Day although I reminded myself that it would be an act of love to do so. Selfishly, I kept him with me one more night, wrapped in his favorite blanket and snuggled against my chest. This one, last evening ritual must suffice for a lifetime. We both were content—he purred and slept quietly as I stroked his soft, downy fur. I dozed, warmed by his fragile body and strong spirit. At dawn, I bundled him up and took him out to watch the wintry sunrise.

The vet asked if I wanted to be there when they euthanized him.

"Of course," I said. "He's spent more time in my lap than my children did."

I could no longer feel Simon's heart beating against my palm. The vet said, "Simon was a great cat." I blinked and nodded mutely. The doctor stroked Simon's paw. "He lived to be an old kitty, older than a lot of cats without feline leukemia.

He purred his way through one injury after another; he's a very gentle, good-natured old boy. When my other patients come in with a kitten or family cat with feline leukemia, certain it must be euthanized, I tell them about Simon and what a good cat he's been all these years. He's sort of a hero to a lot of little kitties out there."

Heroes come in all descriptions—including a fuzzy white cat, with three legs and a crooked smile, named Simon.

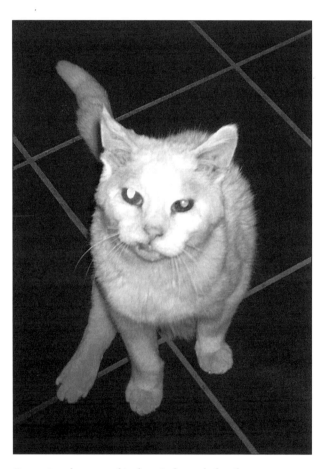

Simon gives the camera his charmingly crooked smile.

About the Author

Carol Downie has a natural bent toward compassion and service, having been a language arts teacher, an instructor for "mutual respect" seminars and a volunteer gardener who worked with vulnerable youth. Aside from her obvious affinity for her domestic animal companions, she indulges her passion for wildlife through outdoor activities. An avid outdoors enthusiast, Carol enjoys wilderness camping, scuba diving, gardening, and, in her new Arizona home, desert and mountain hiking.

Since retiring from her job as a health care administrator, Carol has more time to pursue her writing and literature interests at her home in Fountain Hills, AZ. In the past year, two of her personal essays have been published: "Diving in Hawaii," was published by *Undercurrent Magazine* and "The Red Cup" was published in the initial issue of *Conservation Minnesota* magazine.

The Healing Touch of the Xolos: Pink
Sharon Sakson

Nancy Gordon of San Diego discovered that when she put her Mexican Hairless Dog on her neck or wrist, the heat from the dog's body was strong enough to ease the pain of Nancy's chronic fibromyalgia. She wasn't the first person to discover this.

The dogs have an ancient history as healers. In their native country, Aztecs placed the dogs in their beds, to function as heating pads. They draped them over their necks, knees and hips for relief from arthritis. They named the breed *Xoloitzcuintle*, derived from combining the name of the Aztec Indian god, *Xolotl*, and the Aztec word for dog, *itzcuintle*. The word is pronounced "show-low-eats-queent-lee."

Nancy's first dog, named Toaster because of the warmth she generates, was willing and eager to help Nancy. When Toaster had a litter of puppies, Nancy kept one female she named Pink, for the color of her skin. Pink watched her mother and did what Toaster did, learning to become an even more proficient service dog. She carries things for Nancy, picks up things she has dropped, and helps her undress by tugging off a sleeve or pant leg. Pink works 'round the clock for Nancy, and is happy to do it. Without her, the handicap of fibromyalgia made Nancy's life difficult.

Pink now lives life with a handicap of her own. She developed a slipping patella problem that had to be repaired by surgery. While she was under anesthesia, the veterinarian discovered that some of the bones in her right rear leg had somehow been damaged and had fused together. The vet asked Nancy's permission to remove the leg. Otherwise, every step Pink took would be painful.

Nancy says, "Up to that point in my life, the hardest decision I had ever made was to close my practice. The pain I was experiencing from my injuries every day made it impossible to continue." Nancy had been a licensed Clinical Social Worker, who worked hard counseling her needy patients. She loved her job, but a car accident put an end to that by plunging her into constant pain. Eventually, she was diagnosed with Fibromyalgia (FMS) and Chronic Fatigue Immune System Disorder (CFIDS).

"This decision was the second hardest of my life. I agonized over it because I didn't know if Pink would be able to go on living her life the way she wanted—very active and constantly retrieving things."

In the end, because Pink's health was in jeopardy, Nancy had to agree to the amputation. She waited anxiously in a treatment room a few days after the surgery, eager to take Pink home.

"If I could describe how she looked that day, when she realized her leg was gone…she was mad. It gives me chills to remember how angry she looked. If you can say a dog was livid, she was livid. Poor thing. I felt so sorry for her.

"But she's shown me you don't give up. You get over the handicap and keep on going. Now, she retrieves as well as she ever did. She lives to retrieve. Dogs live so much in the moment. They don't hold grudges. If they get burned by the stove, they learn not to touch the stove again, but they don't get mad at the stove."

Pink went right back to work as Nancy's service dog, ignoring her own terrible handicap. In fact, her appearance is so normal that people meeting her for the first time often don't notice that she's standing on only three legs.

In Nancy's eyes, Pink is the most beautiful dog in the world. Most people meeting Xolos for the first time don't feel that way. The breed is usually the winner of "Ugly Dog" contests. They have hairless, tough skin in black, gray, red, liver or bronze. They are often missing teeth, which can cause their tongues to hang from the side of their mouths. But their winning personalities usually overcome poor first impressions.

Nancy says that Pink is incredibly intelligent and intuitive. She occasionally seems able to anticipate what Nancy needs and brings it before she asks. She is sensitive to Nancy's pain. Sometimes Nancy stays too long at her desk, which causes her body to ache. She'll try to ignore the pain. Then she sees Pink staring at her, with a worried look on her wrinkled little face. She realizes that Pink knows she is in pain and is signaling her, in her own Xolo way, to stop and lie down.

"Pink has shown me that animals are angels for us, healing us in more ways than we can imagine," Nancy says.

Pink has been taught to bring Nancy her cell phone. Now, when Pink hears it ring, she hunts it down as fast as she can and gets it to Nancy in time to take the call. Nancy doesn't ask her to do this: Pink trained herself to respond, and won First Prize in a "Best Trick" contest for that feat.

Nancy says, "Pink loves to be of service. She is so happy to get you anything you want. When she can't figure out what you want, watching her mind work is amazing.

"Once, an important document blew out of my hands and went down the street. I was desperate to get it back but it moved out of reach again. Pink ran over to it, but dogs can't pick paper off the ground. There's nothing to hold on to. She tried several different times, but couldn't get it. Finally, she licked the paper (and it stuck to her tongue) so it came up enough so she could grab it with her teeth. She brought it back without a mark on it."

That's how much Pink wants to be of service.

"I can't imagine my life without my dogs now," Nancy says. "Toaster changed my life, and Pink has become my inspiration. She helped me get out in the world when I was so disabled."

Nancy decided to use her experience to help other people. She formed a non-profit agency to attract funding so that she can breed Xolos and place them with people suffering from chronic pain. As far as she knows, she's the first person to try to build an organization encouraging the use of Xolos as service dogs. She named her mission "X-CPR™," or "Xolos For Chronic Pain Relief."

"Because of constant pain, I thought I'd lost the nurturing

side of me," Nancy recalls. "Pink showed me that I could carry on my life despite my pain, and learn to help others. She's an inspiration not only to me, but to everyone who meets her. It's like she's saying, 'What missing leg? Oh, that. Life is too short to worry about that.'"

For more information on Xolos for Chronic Pain Relief, contact:

X-CPR
c/o Nancy Gordon
Paws for Comfort
P.O. Box 601784
San Diego, CA 92160
Phone 619-599-5228
Fax 619-546-5458
www.pawsforcomfort.com
nancy@pawsforcomfort.com

Owner Nancy Gordon cuddles with her first dog, Toaster, while Toaster's daughter, Pink, wraps herself around Nancy's neck. The warmth of the small, hairless dog eases the ever-present pain caused by Nancy's chronic fibromyalgia.

Pink is so named for her overall coloration. Though she had one of her rear legs amputated, Pink still manages to be of great comfort to her owner, Nancy Gordon.

About the Author

Sharon Sakson is a freelance writer/producer of television programs in New York. She has been a Field Producer for NBC Sports, WNBC, and ABC National News. She produced programs for Court TV, Food TV and local television stations in Baltimore, Chicago and San Francisco. Sharon holds a Master of Fine Arts in Writing degree from the New School for Social Research in New York City. The author of two Bantam travel guides, and writer of more than 100 articles, Sharon's latest project is the popular "Paws" series from Alyson Press. Two 2007 titles—*Paws & Effect: The Healing Power of Dogs* and *Paws & Reflect: A Special Bond Between Man & Dog*—are being followed up this year with *Paws to Protect: Dogs Saving Lives and Restoring Hope.* Sharon is a breeder of champion Whippets, Dachshunds and Brussels Griffons, at her "Parisfield" kennel. She is an accredited American Kennel Club dog show judge, judging most of the hound group and some working breeds.

Inspiration in Our Midst: Ruby
Vicki Tiernan

We are so very lucky to share the planet with them, they who are often our teachers, mislabeled as "lesser beings."

A recent sunny day drew me to Fort Funston, a stunning coastal oasis overlooking the bluffs of the Pacific in northern California, for a leisurely stroll and roll with Ruby, the twelve-year-old Canine American who owns my heart and my deepest admiration. Ruby now roller-commutes on wheels that stand in for rear legs. Those legs, once awesome in their power, are now ravaged by degenerative myelopathy (DM), a disease similar to multiple sclerosis in humans.

On that stroll, we encountered a man who was entranced as he watched "RuRu" sail around on her wheels, ears perked excitedly so as not to miss a single note of the symphony she lives for: ocean, gulls, people.

"Well, nothing's going to keep you down, now is it?" the man exclaimed, as she left him in the dust. He then smiled at me with great warmth and said, "Thanks for getting her out here. She inspires me."

In vast understatement, I replied that she inspires me, too. I get that kind of uplifting remark a lot lately, and with all my heart I wish I could transmit the feeling it brings me to everyone reading this.

As Ruby rolls excitedly past—sometimes over—them along the path to nowhere in particular, folks often get the besotted look of those who have been gently reminded of something very important. Faces soften as they watch her going about her usual doggy pursuits, delighting in the simplest of things and refusing to yield a single iota of her joy to the horrific poison dart life has thrown at her.

"Ah, yes," we remember. "When all else fails, there is still a day in the park, friends and new adventures." There is always this.

DM is a dreadful predator, no question. Given the choice, I of course would have elected for Ruby to evade this horrific bullet, but the disease did strike. Yet, in its destructive wake, we who are lucky enough to know Ruby have been offered a valuable insight on perspective from a most unassuming teacher.

Some folks are apologetic about asking questions they surmise—correctly—I've answered many times before. Truth is, I never tire of talking about Ruby's struggle and how she has met it with plucky persistence at every turn, free-wheeling over virtually every obstacle in her path and acting for all the world like she doesn't even know she's disabled. In the telling of Ruby's story, my own sense of optimism and inspiration reawakens, and it happens each and every time.

In her younger years, Ruby—half Lab, half Dobie—was a blur of wind and rapture. She crested waves of dune at Fort Funston effortlessly, defying all laws of physics and gravity, sheer joy filling every pore. Nothing made her happier than chasing down—at breakneck speed—any object that left my hand and landed elsewhere, anywhere.

When Ruby first became wheel-bound at the age of eleven, I worried that she might feel left out if she saw other dogs chasing Frisbees, her most cherished activity in former days. As it turns out, this is not an issue. Not in the least.

"I'm past that now, Mom," her demeanor seems to say, "and my wheels are just as cool as any Frisbee."

At the same time, Ruby is not above using her new station in life to mooch an obscene array of dog treats on every walk. She rolls on up to smiling passers-by and flashes a look of "How can you *not* give cookies to a dog on wheels?" Works every time.

When we get home from our walks, we negotiate the two flights to my apartment with Ruby walking on front legs, hind end held aloft by me, via a sling under her belly. I think about the level of agility and trust required for her to accomplish this, and it amazes me. Yet we do it at least twice a day every day, my awesome little teammate and I.

Prone to viewing the world all too often through the smoked lens of depression, I feel so grateful for the simple yet profound glimpse of other perspectives offered up by a creature who no doubt will glean gold from her life experience, however limited, to the very last day.

I know that at times, this valuable lesson will be lost in the quagmire of everyday life. The clarity I experience from a meditation sitting often lasts about as far as the ride home. Yet I know also that the picture of the indomitable Ms. Ru rolling gleefully through life will become a golden thread within the fabric of my cosmology, a shining image that will resurface from time to time to remind me anew of what is—when all else falls away—important. In this and many other ways, my little friend and spiritual teacher will live on forever.

Meanwhile, back on the physical plane, I'm reminded often of late that we don't get to play this game for keeps, Ruby and I. It gives me great comfort to know that she's never happier than when exploring new worlds. I hope she will leave her wheels and me behind as easily as she discarded her Frisbees, as she completes her earthly adventure and moves on to explore whatever the next bend in the road might hold. I hope she leaves with the sense that I've given her as much as she has given me.

Creating fitting final tribute to such an extraordinary spirit will be no small challenge. I hope I can find the most eloquent words that ever worked their way to paper. What comes to mind right now is simply to say: Thank you, THANK YOU, Universe, for letting her set with me a spell.

Postscript - Ruby soared gleefully over many a foreboding obstacle in her life. In May of 2002, she met with a hurdle she could not quite clear, and she took the ultimate flight on May 25.

To me, she was the Spirit of San Francisco and then some: funny, sometimes irreverent, always with a gleam in her eye, ready for every new adventure, unstoppable to the very last.

She was earthbound for twelve years, but her spirit touched the stars.

Ruby's idea of playing with sticks.

Ruby flying over the dunes at Fort Funston, California, age two. She would later return to roll over these same hills on her cart. She also thought nothing of going for a stroll in the Mojave Desert.

– Photo by Dan Manchak

About the Author

Vicki Tiernan is a medical transcriptionist who holds a degree in psychology and lives in San Francisco. She writes when something moves her to do so and says that the story of Ruby caused a wellspring from her heart to the page.

Vicki is a former Executive Committee Member of the San Francisco Dog Owners Group and has been an ardent advocate for reasonable park access for off-leash recreation in her hometown. Clearly, honoring relationships between people and their pets is important to Vicki, who says, "We can learn so much from beings so aptly described by Henry Beston as 'other nations, caught with ourselves in the net of life and time, fellow prisoners of the splendour and travail of the earth.'"

The author with her dog, Lula—Ruby's successor.

- Photo by Pat Boyd

Battle for Life: Krieg
Cheryl Caruolo

When my friend Marie saw a newspaper ad that read: *German Shepherd puppies for sale*, she knew the timing was right to get a dog for her daughters—Alison, eleven, and Melissa, who had recently celebrated her ninth birthday.

On the day Marie visited the breeder to choose a puppy, only her older daughter was with her. Alison was drawn to a golden-brown female who seemed more alert than the other eight-week-old pups. While her daughter was distracted playing with the scampering puppies, Marie noticed that there were five in the litter. When she mentioned the count, the breeder averted her eyes a moment. Then she sighed, leaned in and whispered, "The sixth is too weak and the vet told me to put him down, but I don't have the heart."

Marie, who in her youth took in every stray animal she came across, asked to see the sixth puppy. As the breeder escorted her to a back bedroom, Alison was holding the chosen female in her lap and rubbing the tiny belly of another.

The runt of the litter was lying on a flannel baby blanket—his silhouette so thin, only the yellow of the blanket defined him at all. Mostly black with a little touch of tan, his fragile-looking body didn't stir when Marie sat on the bed. His ears were curled up and folded under, his nearly-blind eyes were opaque gray.

The breeder said, "He's not for sale; we'll keep him until he dies. The vet told us he has about four months."

On the heels of the breeder's last syllable, Alison pushed past her mom and jumped on the bed next to the puppy. She paused as she absorbed the appearance of the ill-fated creature, then handed her mom the chosen puppy she was holding and said that she wanted the exiled dog instead. Marie explained that the puppy was on borrowed time. Alison was silent the entire ride home.

A few days later, the breeder called to coordinate a pick-up time for the stalwart female puppy.

"We were really taken with you and your daughter," she said. "The female puppy you chose stands over her tender brother to keep the others from crushing him, and we would prefer that the awkward pup remain with his sister. It'd be better for him. For them. If you are okay with the little time he has, we'd like you to take him."

Marie didn't hesitate at all—she believed that her family could love the malformed puppy more than any other family. And so many animals, from iguanas to goats, had passed through her household, her daughters understood that death was a natural transition of life.

A week later, Marie picked up the brother-sister duo while the girls were in school. When she came home, she called her daughters outside and as she slid open the door of the van, both girls screamed.

"The female is yours Melissa. The male is entrusted to you, Alison."

Her older daughter scooped up the disfigured being and smiled.

Because they were Shepherds, the girls wanted German names. Melissa settled almost immediately on Hildegard—a fitting name, considering the way she watched over her challenged brother—but Alison couldn't decide. Then one day, while she was watching a movie, Alison ran upstairs and announced that her pup's name was Krieg.

"It means 'war' in German," she exclaimed.

Marie had no idea what it meant, but since Krieg was in for a battle, even a counterfeit warrior's name would do.

When the time came for the puppies to get their second series of shots, Marie took Hilde and Krieg to Dr. Josh, a vet she had known for more than a decade.

Dr Josh took a look at Krieg, cocked his head to one side and said, "Interesting cranium." He smiled when Marie told him the story of the unusual shepherd. Then he told her exactly what the first vet had told the breeder. "This puppy is deformed and underdeveloped. He won't live long."

Dr. Josh had great compassion for all animals, and he was delicately trying to prepare Marie for the pending early death of the fraught being.

"I wouldn't bother with the additional inoculations," he cautioned.

Impervious to any nay-saying counsel, she replied, "Give him the same series as Hilde."

Dr. Josh smiled and nodded his head, then gently warned, "You probably shouldn't throw a ball for our delicate guy. Trying to catch it might cause him a heart attack."

Krieg outlasted his four-month sentence and at ten months old, when Marie decided to breed Hildegard, she spoke to the vet about fixing him. Dr. Josh told her the chance of Krieg making it through the surgery was slim.

"Your guy's heartbeat is so irregular, he'll need a cardiologist and specialized monitoring equipment. His frail body may not be able to handle the anesthesia."

With a husband out of work, two young children and a mortgage, Marie did not have the money for sophisticated machinery and expensive doctors.

"Put him under with the least amount of medication to keep him pain-free. If he doesn't wake up," her voice began to crack, "give him a big kiss from me."

Four hours later, Dr. Josh summoned Marie to the office. Her stomach sank.

When the automatic glass doors of the clinic clicked open, the vacuumed air hit Marie's face and she blinked twice to re-focus. Looking down the column-like hallway, she saw Krieg slouched against a metal desk and flanked by two technicians.

She started to cry. "Ohhh, buddy-boy!"

The frozen figure scrambled to its feet and headed down the passage towards Marie's voice. With his back legs going faster than his front and his butt sliding sideways, he looked like an 18-wheeler jack-knifing.

Dr. Josh swallowed hard. "He knows that voice."

As he developed, Krieg's brow protruded, Frankenstein-like. His forehead became overly elongated, and his snout was almost as thin as a tapered candle. His head and chest came to points and his ribs were concave. Marie, familiar with breeding, knew that they would never expand. Through his cloth-thin skin, his heart was visible with every beat. His gums were so receded that his teeth appeared twice as long as other dogs. When he smiled, he looked like a werewolf out of a B movie. A friend teased Marie about sending a photograph of Krieg to inspire Stephen King.

Krieg may have been Alison's pup, but there was a special bond between the canine German soldier and Marie. Perhaps—with her black, scalp-short hair spiked up in random patterns, multiple tattoos and piercings—she knew something about looking different. Because Krieg could only see shadows and bumped into everything, Marie affectionately called him "Forrest Gump."

Over time, there were teaching moments when Marie put a dish of dog food on the floor, then knelt down and stuck her face in the food while Krieg was eating. There were so many neighborhood children, it was her method of insuring that he would never attack anyone who inadvertently got in the way during dinnertime. There were silly moments, like the time the dogs raced to be first into the car. Krieg misjudged the doorframe and fell, his gangly legs flailing every which way, face-first into the van. And there were charmed moments, when Krieg teased Hilde by pushing a plush animal toy into her face, snarling a dare for her to take it from him. Never one to let her baby brother get the best of her, Hilde usually took the challenge, snatching the plaything from her growling sibling. It always made Marie laugh whenever she noticed Krieg feverishly sniffing around to find it again.

But the memory with the sweetest emotional resonance happened over the summer, during a family weekend camping trip. Saturday night included a trip to Dairy Queen, complete with a baby-sized ice cream cone for each dog. As Alison held the cone for Krieg, he closed his eyes to lap it up as if he were a nursing newborn again.

Days slipped into months, summer into autumn, and Krieg grew to look like Jack Nicholson's character in The Shining. About the time the girls were back in school, a third German Shepherd named Fritz joined the crew, and the triad became inseparable. Ironically, the abnormal Krieg was the tallest of the three and established himself as the alpha dog, though Hildegard wouldn't hesitate to shove him back in line if she caught him misbehaving.

Whenever Marie signaled for the squad to come into the house, Krieg would follow Hilde's lead. On the occasions when he was left behind, he twisted his pointy head from side to side, tracking Marie's voice until he found his way to her.

Krieg usually tagged along on any of the other dogs' visits to Dr. Josh. The kindhearted vet always shook his head and chuckled. "Love keeping you alive?"

Almost two years after Krieg first arrived, Fritz and Hilde had a litter of six puppies. The family kept one; the smallest of the pups, with ears that permanently flopped downward, the runt of the litter. Krieg welcomed his odd nephew with personal understanding, and Willie showed his uncle the respect due the leader of the pack. The trio melded seamlessly into a quartet.

One day, Melissa picked up a Frisbee and tossed it to Hilde, who loved to catch things in mid-air. The matriarch of the clan jumped about four feet off the ground and caught the disk as she usually did. Alison, watching from the porch, squealed with excitement and startled Krieg.

Marie remembered Dr. Josh's advice: Trying to catch a ball might kill him. But she figured if Krieg died while leaping for the heavens, at least he'd leave happy. She picked up a neon orange Frisbee and aimed it to hit Krieg softly on the snout.

He blinked, sneezed and stepped forward a bit. Marie retrieved the disk and repeated the toss, again bumping Krieg in the snout. With the third smack, Krieg snapped at the air. On the fourth try, he snagged the side of the plastic with one of his colossal teeth.

The school years passed, the girls grew, and the canine clique protected and played. Every trip to the vet brought the same pleased question. "Love keeping you alive?"

On a cloudy spring day, four years after Hildegard and her misfit brother joined her life, Marie received a call from her neighbor while she was at work.

"You'd better come home," he said. "Something is wrong with one of the dogs."

When she arrived home, Marie found Krieg lying motionless on his side in the middle of the backyard, the neon orange Frisbee to his left, Fritz and Willie sitting to his right, and Hilde straddling him, on guard, as she had done from his tenuous beginning.

Marie buried Krieg in the far left corner of the yard, under the shade of a sixty-year-old maple tree, while the girls were still at school. When she told them Krieg was gone, Melissa hid her face in her mother's chest and sobbed. Alison, now a teenager, walked straight to her room in the same cloak of silence that had insulated her the day she and the petite Shepherd first met. Marie ached to console her, but knew she had to honor the adolescent need to grieve in private.

The next day, from the kitchen window, Marie saw Alison and Hildegard, the ever-faithful shepherd, holding vigil at the gravesite. She noticed Krieg's favorite Frisbee in Alison's hand, and fought the lump building in her throat.

A moment later, Hilde seized the edge of the disk in her mouth as if she was contemplating play. Then she dropped the brightly-colored disk to the ground, and nudged it on top of the still-fresh mound of earth.

All grown up, Krieg (left) found love, trust and joyous companionship with his birth sister, Hildegard. She was very protective of her special brother, and watched over him like a guardian.

About the Author

Cheryl Caruolo, a freelance writer/editor and certified holistic therapist in the Boston area, channels energy through ancient healing arts. She recognizes the parallels between energy work and the healing exchange between animals and humans in a loving relationship. Her affirming story of Krieg proves the power of such energy in overcoming adversity.

Cheryl holds a Master of Fine Arts in Creative Writing degree from Lesley University in Cambridge, MA. While her writing is diverse, she specializes in science, spirituality and personal essay. Her work has appeared in *Reiki News*, *Thereby Hangs A Tale*, *Common Thought* and *Cezzane's Carrot*. Several of her pieces have been national literary contest winners. Currently her essay "Return" is part of the traveling multimedia project *Experiencing the War in Iraq* and her poem "Paradox" is part of the upcoming anthology *Writers on the Train* sponsored by Axiom Art Gallery in Boston.

The Thanksgiving Miracle: Idgie
Mary Shafer

I was 41 years old when a tiny, sickly kitten came into my life. I couldn't have known then what a profound effect she would have on me, and I'm glad now that I didn't. It might have scared me.

At the time my partner, Shelly, worked for a company that services pet supply stores. Many of these chains have agreements with local shelters to display their animals for adoption. It's a neat program, and a fairly successful one.

On a store visit in September of 2002, Shelly came across a small, gray kitten scuttling across the floor near the checkout register. The creature was making its way around a shelf when the store associate appeared.

Shelly asked why the kitten was running loose in the store. The associate explained that she felt sorry for the tiny female, because all her siblings had been adopted and she was now alone. The associate was giving her a rare bit of freedom outside the display cage.

"I can't believe she hasn't been adopted," Shelly remarked. "She's so cute, and obviously playful."

"No one wants a blind kitten," the associate explained. "She was born that way."

"No way!" Shelly replied, incredulous. She watched the critter tooling around the floor at breakneck speed, obviously unimpeded by any disability.

"Really," the associate assured. She scooped up the kitten and turned its head toward Shelly, who then saw the two empty, pink sockets where its eyes should have been.

At first, Shelly was taken aback—it is kind of an eerie sight if you've never seen such a thing—but as she watched the kitten exploring and playing, then picked it up to pet, she noticed its outgoing personality. The little fuzzball was so sweet-natured that Shelly soon got over her initial shock.

The associate explained that she had found the kitten in downtown Philadelphia on an unseasonably hot day. This gray girl had been in bad shape; starving and dehydrated, with matted fur and flea infestations. She was so far gone that she'd almost become one with the baking hot concrete sidewalk, and maggots had already embedded themselves in her flesh. The associate had taken pity on her, and—a habitual rescuer—gathered her up in a blanket and took her home.

The associate nursed her back to health until she was ready to be shown for adoption. Her rescuer had named the kitten "Magoo," after the notoriously blind cartoon character. She had shaved off the kitten's matted coat to allow for thorough cleaning, and had picked her clean of pests. The fur had since grown back to about half an inch long.

Within minutes, Shelly was smitten. Breaking one of her self-imposed, cardinal rules about working in pet stores, Shelly decided to adopt the kitten. That's when she called me.

I was working at my computer when the call came in. I listened to her story of little "Magoo." Would it be all right to bring the kitten home, Shelly wondered? It was a big commitment and might be a lot of trouble.

"Are you kidding?" I answered. "Bring her home. I can't wait!"

But I had to wait, and tried to concentrate on my work until I heard the door open. I was downstairs in a flash.

Shelly had prepared us well. Considering that the kitten might need a place to feel safe, she had purchased a very large cage. It was roomy enough for a Labrador retriever to inhabit comfortably, with a soft, thick sheepskin pad for the bottom. She and the associate had cut down a shipping carton and lined it with a garbage bag for use as a litter box.

We set up the cage in my office, where we could shut the doors to keep the new kitten apart from both our other cats until she was ready for company. A couple bowls filled with food and water, a few playthings from our overflowing cat toy basket, and it became a serviceable home for our newest family member.

I remember being almost afraid to touch the kitten the first time Shelly handed her to me. Her little belly was still distended from malnutrition and ravaging by intestinal parasites. In places, her short hair was clotted with sweat, and there were those…sockets. Those pink, moist membranes were like window shades that had been pulled down over her eyes, only there were no eyes.

The first thing we agreed was that the kitten's name had

to go. Though humorous, "Magoo" seemed to define her by her disability. And clearly, this little dynamo was not handicapped in the least by her lack of visual organs.

Shelly knew I had always admired the gutsy, courageous lead character played by Mary Stuart Masterson in the movie "Fried Green Tomatoes," and suggested we name the kitten after her.

I agreed. Our newest "child" would be named Idgie.

I took her in my arms and sat back on the futon in my office. Idgie remained on her back, cradled against my chest for a moment. Then—for the first of thousands of times—she arched her back until her tiny body formed an almost perfect C. Her back legs were splayed out behind her, and the abnormally round, white belly protruded in front.

Then, to my surprise and delight, she reached her front paws up and touched my face. I looked down. Her mouth, with its minute gray lips, seemed drawn up in a smile. Her whisker disks formed fuzzy white "poofs" on either side. She was holding my face between her paws, and I could feel the warmth of her soft, gray toes on my chin and cheeks.

That was it. I was utterly undone.

I've had pets all my life and have loved them all, some more deeply than others. But this one had captured my heart with her spunky spirit and obvious joy in simply being alive. From that point on, I have never been the same, and now it's a joke with my friends and family that she has me wrapped around her little white paw.

Within minutes, we placed a call to Dr. Ellen Prieto, our wonderful rural vet. She was able to see us right away. The doc was fascinated with Idgie, exploring the possibility that she actually had eyeballs we just couldn't see. Ellen thought perhaps Idgie's nictitating membrane simply hadn't developed enough to pull away properly. In a few moments, though, Ellen had assured herself and us that there were, indeed, no eyeballs hidden behind that pink flesh.

We soon got past the disappointment, simply glad that the endearing critter seemed healthy despite her ordeal. However, Ellen wanted to be sure Idgie hadn't been exposed to any of the contagious diseases that run rampant among feral cats. She tested her for feline leukemia, giving the test time to process while she completed the physical examination.

Ellen checked Idgie's ears, reporting that we'd have to begin a regimen of regular ear washing to get rid of the bothersome mites that had taken up residence. We also learned that she had contracted ringworm, which would require frequent daily washings with strong antibacterial soap. We would need to regularly dose her eye sockets with artificial tears to keep the membranes properly lubricated.

All the while, Idgie proceeded to charm Dr. Ellen with her playfulness. Ellen was amazed at the energy she had for still being so sick. When she finished the physical, Ellen reached for the test vial waiting on her lab table. As soon as we saw her face, we knew the results weren't good.

She looked gravely at us and said, "Girls, I'm sorry. It's positive."

"Are you sure?" we asked. "Maybe you should run it again."

"This is a very accurate test. I can run it again if you want me to, but I'm certain the outcome will be the same, and then I'll have to charge you for another one."

We looked at each other, our hearts sinking.

Ellen reminded us that Idgie would have to be kept separate from Tigger and Weaver, our other cats, and that they must have no physical contact with her at all. We'd have to make Idgie's status as official mascot of my writing business permanent.

Dr. Ellen then turned to us and said, very solemnly, "I must warn you not to expect to have her for very long. FeLeuk is an untreatable and fatal disease, and she's so young. Her health is compromised already, so…"

"So how long do you think we can expect her to live?" I asked, bluntly.

Ellen took a deep breath, and looked toward Idgie. She ran a gentle hand over the tiny head and back.

"A year, maybe. It could be longer, but I wouldn't expect that."

Again, Shelly and I exchanged sorrowful glances and the tears rose, but we didn't cry. There really wasn't any point. The situation was what it was. We knew when we took her out of that pet store the commitment we were making, and the risks attached to it.

But Ellen, as always, asserted her faith in the power of her practice, even in the face of this sad news.

"We'll put her on a regimen of vitamins and supplements to help make her as strong as we can, along with an immune booster to help her fight off any further infections. This way, we'll make sure you can have her with you as long as possible." She proceeded to gather some bottles and droppers to send home with us, adding, "At least whatever life she has from now on will be happy, because it's clear you love her already."

With lumps in our throats, we thanked the doctor and returned home, much more soberly than we had arrived. On the drive back, we discussed the ramifications of this medical revelation. We agreed it would be hard—for Idgie and for us—to keep her apart from her adopted brothers, but resigned ourselves to doing so. There was simply no other option.

When we got in the door, our two "boys" were very curious. It was hard not to let them sniff their new sister and get to know her. We headed straight up the steps. I think the boys believed we were playing some kind of hide-and-seek game, because they both exhibited that playful slinkiness cats do when they think you're teasing them. It was difficult to shut the door in their curious faces.

Shelly and I put Idgie into the cage, watching her pick a spot and lie down. She was exhausted from her adventurous day. We discussed the logistics of keeping her world the size of one room. We were very sad, both that she wouldn't be able to play with the boys, and that we wouldn't have her for long. We had both fallen completely under Idgie's spell, and had already begun to imagine the loss we would feel. But we agreed that everything happens for a reason, that we were obviously chosen to take on this responsibility. We would love her as much as we could for as long as we could, and make her life as happy as possible for whatever time we were given together.

The first few nights, I slept on the futon in my office, so Idgie could hear me breathing and not be afraid because she was alone in a strange place. Sometimes, I'd leave her cage door open and bring her on the chair with me, where she would curl up against me or on top of my chest, and go to sleep with her head tucked into the curve of my neck.

I've never had children, but I imagine the love and protectiveness I felt swelling inside for her had to be akin to that a mother feels for her newborn. I never slept very well, because I was afraid I might roll over on her or do some other damage, but I treasured those nights when she sought me out and trusted me to keep her safe and warm.

Almost two months went by, and we fell into a routine of washing and combing and dosing Idgie with her many medications and supplements. Gradually, she began to gain a little weight. Her distended stomach shrunk to a normal size, and she could now stay awake long enough to play with us for a bit each day.

Our older cat, Tigger, grew weary of wondering what we'd secreted in my office, and gave up trying to find out. Weaver, on the other hand, was still very much a kitten himself. He was frisky and needed a playmate more energetic and tolerant than Tigger, so Weaver routinely laid just outside my office doors, which in our old house don't go all the way to the floor.

It wasn't a problem as long as Idgie remained weak and hadn't recovered enough to leave the cage much. But soon, she had regained her strength and was becoming a real cat, showing signs of the fabled curiosity. Within a week or so, she had regained enough muscle tone to begin taking short walks outside the cage.

Like any good patroller, the first thing she established in her sightless world was a mind's-eye map of its perimeter. Through constant circuits of the room's boundaries, she established for herself a thorough schematic of its outline, obstacles and different surface levels. She was still too small to jump up on the futon by herself, so when she reached that part of her circuit, I'd lift her up and set her on it. I did so slowly, so she could gain a sense of how high off the floor she was moving. She would sniff and paw and walk all over it until she had it memorized. I imagined I was watching a mobile Braille sensor at work.

When she reached the doors, at first she would softly bump into them. She wasn't moving fast enough for it to hurt, and her body had adapted to her lack of sight by making itself less vulnerable to harm should she take a tumble. Even taking into account the fact that she was still very young, her legs were proportionately about half the length of her brothers'. At first, we thought perhaps this was a function of her youth, but even as she grew they remained in that proportion.

We also noticed that her lateral whiskers—the ones radiating from her snout—were nearly twice as long proportionately as those of other cats. These two physical adaptations gave her a better "sonar" through extra-long feelers, and a shorter distance before hitting the floor should she slip or fall.

After finalizing the survey of her physical surroundings, Idgie got around almost as well as a sighted cat.

One day, Weaver was lying in the hallway just outside the door as usual. He must have made a noise, because Idgie stopped short just in front of the door. She slunk down and began sniffing at the crack below it. Weaver apparently saw or heard this, because he extended one of his snow-white paws underneath to see if he could get a reaction. He knew she was in the room, and was terribly curious.

Before I could get to the door to stop it, Idgie had shot her paw under the door to "catch" whatever was making the sound she heard. She just missed Weaver's paw, and he thought she was playing a game. Suddenly, they both started doing this hilarious, fast-motion paw slapping. It was so cute I almost let them go on doing it, but I knew it was too dangerous for Weaver. Sadly, I had to separate them, but that started a game that, to this day, has never ended.

As Idgie grew larger and healthier, her coat grew back. We realized she wasn't a shorthair at all, but a longhair of the most luxurious variety. She developed the classic ruff that so often haloes the heads of longhairs, making them appear lionesque. Her white underbelly hair grew long, as did her overall blue-gray coat. It requires brushing every few days, and when we finish, she looks regal. When she runs or even walks quickly, her coat pops up and down on her body the way a person riding a horse posts. Her tail is now so full that, when she's excited or scared, it fuzzes out to such roundness that we've come to refer to this phenomenon as "Christmas tree tail." With this fuller coat, the small, thin patch of white connecting her chin and chest patches became more visible against the deep gray background. We call it "the milk drip."

As she got stronger, Idgie became more curious about her surroundings, clearly aware there was more to the house than just my office. After a few weeks, she took to standing in front of the hallway door and either shoving her stubby front leg under it as far as she could reach, or meowing to be let out.

We couldn't just let her run loose, but we knew we had to figure out a way to let her explore more of the house. She was blind, but there was nothing wrong with her sharp mind. She was bored.

Shelly and I decided to try an experiment. We went downstairs to our shared studio space and closed the swinging door from the back kitchen. We also closed the pair of French doors dividing the studio from the living room. Through their glass, her brothers could see Idgie without being able to touch her, because the doors go almost all the way to the floor. In the one place they don't, I secured the gap with a length of clear packing tape. Then we brought down Idgie's sheepskin pad (she had pretty much abandoned the cage), her food and water bowls, and her litter box.

At first, it was a little scary for all of us. We were afraid Idgie might find something to hurt herself on, and I think she was a little wary herself. But soon she was toodling around, happily exploring the many nooks and crannies of her new room. We couldn't leave her there overnight, in case she would get into trouble. The two-foot-thick stone walls in our pre-Civil War era farmhouse don't allow us to hear much past whatever room we're in, and we wouldn't know if she was calling for help. So she stayed there during the day, and we could watch her either from inside the room or out in the living room. At bedtime, she returned to the safe familiarity of my office.

Still, Idgie and Weaver tried to play with each other, and it was a pitiful sight to watch them struggle to touch. Once in awhile, one or the other of them would get truly frustrated and let out a sad cry. It was so hard to take. We often talked about how hard it was going to be to keep them separated throughout Idgie's life, however short it might be.

Shelly's mother came to visit in September, and got a big kick out of watching Idgie's antics. Like all kittens, Idgie was tremendously playful and energetic, never running out of ways to amuse herself and us. We watched her play with myriad items; balls of paper, plastic bags and cardboard boxes. We kept her supplied with these things, hoping it would stave off the onset of complete boredom with her enforcedly small world.

Months rolled by, and slowly Idgie's afflictions faded. The ear mites were defeated through daily swabbing, and the ringworms disappeared as we completed the disinfectant regimen. Her coat had completely filled in, and she was now staying awake and active most of the day.

After several checkups, Dr. Ellen pronounced her as healthy as she was going to get. We were thrilled with her progress, but it was never far from our minds that we couldn't allow ourselves to feel too optimistic. "Healthy," for Idgie, was a limited term.

Idgie was the only one who didn't get this message. She continued to grow stronger and more energetic by the day. Her playful, happy demeanor kept our worries at bay. Even when working away at the bottom of a door, trying to make contact with her brother, she was clearly enjoying herself. It was amazing to watch, and I didn't miss the message. I found myself more often feeling grateful for all my good fortune, and whining less when things didn't go my way.

Still, we were the ones who now became frustrated. It was so hard to believe this frisky creature, whose life had become so robust, was going to succumb to an awful, unseen disease one day in the not-too-distant-future.

I couldn't accept it. I told Shelly I simply did not believe the cat was going to die. Idgie didn't act at all afflicted, and something about her indomitable spirit affected mine. As much faith as I had in Dr. Ellen's knowledge and abilities, I had spent nearly every waking moment with Idgie since she'd arrived. I'd played with her, watched her and held her. I'd sat with her on my lap or around my neck while I worked at the computer for hours on end. I was very closely attuned to her, and lately had begun to feel that something had changed; that Idgie wasn't sick anymore.

Though I knew it was probably just wishful thinking, I couldn't shake this thought. It haunted me all the time. Finally, I told Shelly I thought we should question Ellen's pronounced death sentence. Shelly agreed that Idgie seemed to have changed drastically, admitting she, too, had a problem believing the kitten was terminally ill. Still, she cautioned me against hoping for too much. She knew how attached I had become to Idgie, and didn't want to see me get really hurt.

Just before Thanksgiving, I called Ellen. She still makes house calls, and I asked if she was planning to be up our way any time soon. It just so happened she was, so I told her my thoughts. I wanted her to re-test Idgie for feline leukemia.

Ellen was quiet for a moment, then reminded me that there were only very few cases of cats who had originally tested positive later testing negative, and that none of them were documented or conclusive. All such evidence was anecdotal, claims made by non-researchers who couldn't prove them. She, too, was trying to spare me pain.

I appreciated her concern, but I wasn't changing my mind. Everything in my being told me that Idgie was a healthy animal who would live to a ripe, old age. I wanted to prove it, so we could allow her to interact fully with her siblings and not be lonely at night, or ever. Risking our own pain would determine the quality of Idgie's life from now on. It was no time to be faint-hearted.

Finally, Ellen agreed to re-test, and we made an appointment.

I didn't sleep well that night, wondering what the outcome would be. I kept imagining how it would be if Idgie were able to join Tigger and Weaver with us on the bed at night. How she would interact with the boys, and how they would respond to her. How her world would open up. And, I must admit…how it would be not to have to keep a litter box in my office any more.

I woke early the day of the appointment, fed the boys and Idgie. Shelly, too, was anxious, but she had to be on the road for work and wouldn't get home until evening. I promised to call her right away when I got the news, good or bad.

By the time Ellen arrived, I was fidgety and on edge. She apologized for having forgotten to pack the test kit that morning, which meant I'd have to wait for the results until she got back to her office. I thought I would lose my mind from the anxiety.

She examined Idgie as usual, checking her heartbeat, feeling around for anything abnormal. Then finally, she drew some blood while I held Idgie, who only squirmed a little. It was like she knew she had to go through this for something good to happen. Maybe I was just projecting my own hopes, but it really did seem that way to me.

As Ellen left, she promised to call as soon as she had results, but cautioned me again not to get my hopes up. I agreed, but of course I was lying. It was way too late for that. My hopes had been building since before I'd made the appointment.

I tried to concentrate on work while the minutes dragged by. All morning long, I must have glanced at the clock every ten minutes, hoping the phone would ring. When it finally did, around lunchtime, I had gotten myself so wound up that I nearly jumped out of the chair. Caller ID told me it was Ellen, and I snatched the receiver up on the first ring.

"Hello?"

A short silence. Then, simply:

"Miracles do happen."

For an instant, I didn't comprehend, then quickly regained my composure.

"Are you sure?"

"I ran the test twice," replied Ellen. "She's negative."

We both proceeded to whoop and holler. I don't even remember the whole conversation, but I do recall saying that this Thanksgiving would be the most special I'd ever had.

"You're absolutely sure," I repeated, unable to believe the news I'd waited so long to hear. "I can let her out of the room, around the boys?"

"Yes, you can!"

I wept with joy, thanking Ellen profusely. I was so grateful for her insistence on aggressive care for Idgie, her uncommon quest for the latest knowledge about new and alternative therapies, and her belief that perhaps the impossible could happen. And it had.

As soon as I hung up, I dialed Shelly's cell phone, so thankful when she picked up.

"Well?"

"Miracles do happen." I repeated Ellen's mantra, which I would never forget.

"What?" Shelly demanded. "Really?"

"Yes! She tested twice, and said she's convinced Idgie's

negative. No antibodies showed up. She's not sick any more! I'm going to let her out with the boys as soon as I get off this phone."

I don't really remember the rest of that conversation, either, but I know Shelly came home early that day. And ever since, we've referred to Dr. Prieto as "Ellen, the Wonder Vet."

Thanksgiving of 2002 was, indeed, very special. Idgie was the main headline in our holiday newsletter, and she just about cuted us to death discovering the Christmas tree. I took several photos of her lying beneath it, because for me, the symbolism was strong. She was truly my best present that year, and continues to be one of the greatest gifts I have ever received.

Idgie is so much more than a pet. I don't know if it has anything to do with her lack of physical vision, but she carries with her this aura of spiritual wisdom that I have never experienced in an animal (and in few humans). She has comforted me when I have struggled with loss, difficult choices, stressful situations and other unpleasant things. She has been a marvelous friend and confidante, and a reliable companion.

She often lies across my shoulders, along the top of my office chair, while I write. When I encounter a difficult passage or a transition just won't come, I read my material to her, and then shut up and think about it. The answer may take some time, but it always comes. I have never really believed in writer's block, but as long as I have Idgie as my muse, I will never fear its presence in my writing space.

I'm writing this to share the revelations her presence has brought to my life. Watching her negotiate the difficulties her sightlessness has wrought, I am constantly awed and humbled.

I have always admired true courage, and though I believe I'm a fairly skillful writer, I cannot express the immensity of that which Idgie shows every single day. Through it all, she exhibits what I can only describe as joy, in its purest form. This little cat just loves being alive, and she approaches every situation with the intent to squeeze maximum enjoyment out of it.

She is my blessing, this little blind cat. She no longer inspires pity in me, but instead, humility and gratitude. We should all be so lucky. To watch Idgie live her life—jumping from high places with the belief she'll land safely, charging into a room without knowing what's ahead—is to understand what faith really is.

Though I don't pray in the traditional sense of the word, I do communicate in my own way with that energy or being I believe to be the Spirit from which we all emerged and to which we shall return. If I ask for anything, it is to achieve a state of grace.

One book of wisdom says, "Seek, and ye shall find." For me, that phrase embodies the meaning of Idgie in my life. I have been seeking grace, and I believe that she is a guide sent to help me find it. What's amazing is that, with her help, I'm not finding it from somewhere outside myself, but from within.

I know some people will read this and think I'm crazy or sacrilegious. That's okay. We all come to our truth in different ways, and I think each of us only gets those lessons our minds are capable of wrapping themselves around. I guess my mind was flexible enough to realize I could learn a few things from a creature supposedly "subordinate" to me in the big scheme of things. Yeah, right.

There is a saying among followers of ancient spiritualities: "When the student is ready, the teacher appears." I believe this with all my heart. I also believe that we must not have preconceived notions about what form that teacher will take.

Apparently, I passed that readiness test, because never in all my mental ramblings would I have imagined that one of the greatest teachers I'd ever have would be a small, gray cat with no eyes.

Idgie romps and plays right along with her sighted feline siblings. She even participates in scamper chases feline owners will recognize as the "kitty crazies," running full-bore through the house, up and down the stairs.

About the Author

Mary A. Shafer is a fulltime free-lance writer who works from her home in rural Bucks County, Pennsylvania. Her first book, *Wisconsin: The Way We Were, 1845-1945*, was published in 1993 by Heartland Press when she lived in that Midwestern state. That was followed in 1995 by *Rural America: A Pictorial Folk Memory*, from Willow Creek Press in 1995. She took a hiatus to teach commercial art and copywriting at Milwaukee Area Technical College, her alma mater, before moving back to her home state in 1997. 2005 saw the publication of Mary's third book, *Devastation on the Delaware*. Mary is a longtime member of the Humane Society of the United States (HSUS), the American Society for the Prevention of Cruelty to Animals (ASPCA), and the Pennsylvania Society for the Prevention of Cruelty to Animals (PSPCA). She is also the volunteer Weather Coordinator for her hometown's Emergency Management Agency, which can be responsible for aiding in the rescue and care of domestic animals and livestock in emergency situations.

A Shot of Undiluted Love: Arrow
Stacy Ewing

As you enter the driveway, your eyes can hardly take in the varied display of yard embellishments. Colorful plastic carousel rocking horses nestle in the trees on either side of the passage. Twinkling glass sculptures made from recycled lamps, shiny mosaic paving stones, pink flamingoes, and plumbers' pipe mobiles flash like pinball lights. Picnic tables covered with potted house plants compete with the borders of iris and hosta. Dog barks, turkey gobbles, chicken clucks, and horse whinnies give sound effects to the visual jumble.

This is the domain of my friend and dog groomer extraordinaire, Wendy. Her yard is just the first glimpse into her philosophy of life, which is that essentially, there is a place for everything and every creature. She recycles from the dump. She makes sure every patient at the nursing home has a regular visitor. She rescues animals. Wendy takes it all on at full blast and follows through to the end, a guardian angel here on earth.

This is one of her rescue stories.

A few years ago, while Wendy was driving on the outskirts of town, she noticed two dogs ambling along the side of the road. As she got closer, she noticed that they looked pretty scruffy and there were broken chains dangling from their necks. One seemed to be a Lhasa-Apso and the other was some kind of spaniel mix. She stopped the car and opened her door slightly to see if they would come towards her. The dogs shied away from her, so she wasn't going to press the issue. Their coats were matted and they were obviously uncared for, but they didn't run or growl when she called to them. Maybe there was some hope of helping them.

Wendy thought it would be best to have the professionals from Animal Control attempt the capture instead of putting herself at risk, so she put in a call. By the next day, the officers had not been able to locate the dogs. Wendy went out to the last place she had seen them and dumped a bag of dog food. After a few hours, she got a call from the shelter that the dogs had been safely recovered. They asked if she would come down and clean up the shabby runaways.

When Wendy got to the shelter and finally had the chance to meet the two buddies, she was happy to see that, in spite of whatever trials they had been through, they were sweet-natured and friendly. The animal control officers had been able to get the broken pieces of chains from their necks, but no collars or identification were found. And they sure needed a bath! Wendy easily led them to the covered back of her truck and transported them to her grooming shop.

The Lhasa seemed to be in good shape but Wendy noticed that the spaniel was limping a little, so she put him right up on the table to check him over. As she lifted him up, her hands felt large indentations on both sides of his body.

What the heck? she wondered. As she pushed away the matted fur for a better look, she was shocked to find holes as big as her fist in each flank! She got right to work shaving the fur around the wounds and bathing the dog. She could not believe how sweet and docile he was during all this handling. He didn't growl or carry on, not even once. As soon as she had finished, she bundled him up and drove him down to the animal hospital, all the time wondering what in the world could have caused such an injury.

Dr. Shriver examined the dog right away and called for Wendy to come in the back. He showed her the gash on one side and asked her if she could identify the shapes on the edges of the hole. She told him they looked like triangles.

He said, "You're right. Do you know what would cause such an entry mark? An arrow! This poor dog was shot straight through, at close range, with a hunting arrow. The miracle is that it went right through and didn't hit any organs. His heart is fine, his lungs are fine, but he is going to require a lot of care to get well."

The vet told her that he had contacted the shelter and was told they could not commit to the care that the dog would need. He would probably have to put him down.

"I don't care what it takes, I'm going to nurse him back!" Wendy cried, the tears pouring forth. "And from now on, his name is Arrow!"

Thus began a great friendship and many months of attentive care. Arrow required antibiotics four times a day and hot compresses three times a day, which Wendy faithfully administered. Arrow was the perfect patient, never complaining or nipping, but after a few weeks Wendy noticed swelling around his body towards the chest. She took him to the vet and sure enough, there was infection.

The doctor told her she was going to have to keep the compresses on longer and to use a lot of pressure. She took Arrow home and got right to work. By that evening, a lot of the infection had oozed out from the wounds and she knew then that he was going to be okay.

Arrow gazed at her with such love, as if to say, "Thanks."

After about three months, Arrow was well enough to go to the shelter for a newspaper interview and to visit his lhasa buddy, whom Wendy had dubbed Bow. They were celebrities, Bow and Arrow, and Wendy used the opportunity to try to get them adopted together. As close as she had grown to Arrow, she felt the two should be together. That, and her house was already pretty full with five dogs.

What will be, will be, she thought. Within the week, a family came in and adopted Bow. They weren't able to take Arrow, so he stayed on with Wendy. She didn't really want to give him up anyway. It's just that her fiancé was wondering if there was going to be enough room in the house for him!

Life settled down and soon it was as though Arrow had always been there. He still had a twisty limp but, all in all, he had made a nice recovery.

Have you heard it said that certain dogs come into your life just when you need them most? Wendy told me that she cried as she sat and thought about how Arrow had felt when the shaft ripped through his defenseless body. How bad the burning pain must have hurt, how helpless and afraid he must have been. And still, as he bears the scars and loss of mobility, he has such dignity and love for humans. No whining, no angst, no nervousness, no grudge…just sweetness and affection. What an example to have, just before getting married!

As the wedding day approached, Wendy needed to take a trip to her elderly parents' home, so they could meet her fiancé before the ceremony. She had to make arrangements for the care of all her animals while she would be gone, and asked her friend, Janice, to keep Arrow. In retrospect, Wendy's angel wings must have been flapping wildly when she made that connection, since it turned out to be more a case of Arrow keeping watch over Janice.

Janice has a horse farm she acquired through her winnings from a sulky race. Her husband, Frank, lived for sulky racing. He devoted all his time to the tracks or making sure the horses and equipment were in shape. Janice always felt that his compulsion was unhealthy. It was as though he was in a great hurry to keep an appointment with racing destiny. She worried that he never took time to relax or think about anything else. He was so uptight that his skill as a driver became affected. When their finances got low, he would grudgingly ask Janice to drive in races. She could win.

This was the human relationship that Arrow came to. Of course, he could sense the tension in that household but, as usual, he didn't accept any bad feelings. His soul was way beyond mere human dysfunction, far beyond a mere arrow.

Frank, typically preoccupied with racing, hardly acknowledged the dog. Arrow just sat and gazed at him as if to say, "I'm here if you need me." Janice, however, immediately recognized a kindred spirit.

Have you heard it said that certain dogs come into your life just when you need them most? God only knows all the abuses and neglect that Arrow had experienced in his life, but somehow he was given the grace and courage to persevere. Somehow he knew there was a higher purpose to his life, and that all he had to do was, simply, love.

Janice looked into Arrow's soft brown eyes and said, "You and me, kid." The moment was ripe with the knowledge of unconditional acceptance and whatever that intangible thing is that makes us feel absolutely comfortable.

Arrow's smooth red fur, sleek head, and soft, silky ears were so soothing to pet. The indents on his body from the arrow were so dear. Janice thought, *I'm going to softly stroke all your pain away.* She had found a companion to whom she could entrust her affection, knowing it would be completely returned. Arrow had found his purpose.

Their days developed into a routine of lighthearted togetherness. In the morning they walked, fed the horses, took care of correspondence and household chores. When Janice returned from going out, Arrow would be in the same spot as when she left. He didn't run to her, but would gently lift his head. His eyes were shining and his tail was wagging as if to say, "I missed you!" In the evening, when she would sit next to him on the couch, he would tenderly press against her side and accept his ration of petting. No drama, simply love.

Meanwhile, Frank was coming and going, his world consumed with thoughts of racing.

By the time Wendy returned, Janice and Arrow were

entrenched. Janice was prepared to make a plea to keep the dog, but before she could say a word, Wendy said, "So, are you keeping him?"

Janice was overjoyed and agreed. "How did you know I'd want him?" she asked.

Wendy replied that she just had a feeling.

Within the week, Frank let Janice know that the most important race of the season was to be held that weekend. He told her he would be driving and that he had a plan to win.

He had been training a certain horse for months and was ready to carry out his plan. He told her to watch the race carefully. He would be starting out in the rear and would gradually move up until he was behind the four leaders. At the last turn, he would get on the outside and pass those four, then moving to the inside to lead. From there, he would go on to win.

On the day of the race, Janice was watching from the stands and everything went along just as Frank said. She watched as he lengthened his lead, when suddenly Frank just toppled off the sulky and fell over the inside rail. She saw him lying still in the grass, as his horse crossed the finish line in first place. She ran through the stands and down to the field, reaching Frank just as the paramedics arrived. She watched, stunned, as they tried to revive him, but after a few minutes it was clearly no use. Frank was dead. He had had a heart attack within sight of his first win.

As Janice watched them take his body away, she felt numb from the shock and finality of it all. She went through the motions of getting the horse and sulky ready for transport. She answered questions as best she could. She just wanted to get home.

Finally, she was able to leave. It felt so odd to be driving the truck and trailer by herself. She was beginning to get a glimmer of understanding that she was really alone. The thought was too painful, so she quickly pushed it away. She just concentrated on her driving, holding on to the numbness.

When she arrived home, she quickly got the horse settled, then went to the house and opened the door. There was Arrow. Same spot as when she left. Same head lift, eye shine, tail wag. When Janice saw him, the tears came as she hugged his warm, comforting body. The numbness evaporated and her emotions poured over Arrow. Arrow just loved. No drama, simply love.

Arrow had found his purpose.

Have you heard it said that certain dogs come into your life just when you need them most?

Arrow survived his wound to develop into a healthy, happy farm dog.

Wendy and Arrow

About the Author

A lifelong resident of metro Washington, DC, Stacy Ewing is currently a dental sales representative and a freelance writer. She has had articles published in various professional journals in the dental field, and is now expanding her repertoire. Stacy believes that eventually, everyone can find their life's purpose if they follow their hearts. She found her true calling as a writer after a 25-year career as a dental hygienist. She learned the story of Arrow from his real-life rescuer, Wendy, a full-time guardian angel on Earth and a dog groomer in her spare time. She's grateful for the chance to share the life-affirming message she learned from Arrow and Wendy through *Almost Perfect*.

A Most Remarkable Muse: Cagney
Crystal S. Parsons

"How about a rabbit?" asked the teenaged clerk at the local pet store.

"Too smelly."

"Perhaps a ferret?"

"A fuzzy garden hose with teeth? No thanks!"

"I know…what about a rat?"

"A WHAT?!"

The sales clerk had to be joking. Who owns vermin as a pet?

"Stay right there, I have just the thing!"

My husband and I had come in looking for a small pet, something to keep me company while I struggled to finish my thesis in our small apartment.

"Here!" the clerk said, plunking a small, furry rodent into my hands.

He was a full-grown rat, brown and white, and he sat in my hands with his paws clinging to my thumbs. He didn't struggle, just blinked at me, looking slightly bewildered at all the commotion around him.

I blinked back, completely speechless. I was holding a RAT! We stayed like that for a few moments, each of us holding the other, neither one sure what to do with the other.

"Poor little thing has a sad story," said the clerk, finally.

Really, I thought, *what's HIS problem?*

"His owner brought him in for boarding since she was going out of town, but she refuses to pick him up. We're trying to find a good home for him. He's all alone and the stress is causing him to have nosebleeds."

The little rat shifted until he became a small, furry ball in my hands. I held him a little closer for a better look. His markings reminded me of a milano cookie and he had large, bright brown eyes that gave him an intelligent look.

"What's that noise he's making?" I asked, as he started making a small crunching sound.

"He's bruxing. That's the noise a rat makes when it's really happy," she explained. "He likes you!"

Good grief! I thought. *How did I come to this?* But then again, he was kind of cute—little pink nose, little pink ears and those bright, shining eyes.

"Well," I said, looking right into them, "you're lonely and I'm lonely. Let's go home together!"

It wasn't until we brought him home that we noticed something wasn't quite right.

"Honey, come here…there's something wrong with your rat," called my husband.

I went to where he had placed the rat we'd just named Cagney on the coffee table.

"Just watch the way he walks," my husband said.

I sat on the floor until I was eye level with the table, and it was then I noticed it. Cagney seemed to shuffle, his body low to the ground, front legs grasping and pulling. His hind legs moved and pushed a little, but didn't seem to be moving quite right.

"Hmm. I wonder what's wrong with him?" I said. I sat down on the sofa, placed Cagney on my lap and started to stroke his head and back. "I guess it would be a good idea to take him to a vet anyway, you know, just to make sure he's in good health…and see what's wrong with his legs," I prattled on. "I wonder where you find a vet for a rat anywa…"

"Honey, look!" interrupted my husband.

I looked down. The rat had pushed himself up on his front legs and stretched his head up as high as it could get, pushing it into my hand as if trying to get every last sensation of my hand on his head. His eyes were squeezed shut as if he was in some sort of heavenly rapture, enjoying every moment of my touch.

"My god!" I exclaimed. "This poor little thing is just starved for attention!"

He was making that bruxing noise again, only louder this time. If there was anything that could be done for him, I knew we had to try.

I later left the vet's office feeling enraged and miserable. It turned out that Cagney had virtually no muscle in his hindquarters at all.

"How did that happen?" I had asked.

"Well, it's difficult to say, but if his previous owners kept him in a cage too small to move around in, it's possible they never developed properly."

I was livid. How could someone do that to an animal? I mean, to some people Cagney may be just a rodent, but his is still a life. And life is precious, even if it comes in a very small package.

"There is one thing we could try that might help," suggested the vet.

When I explained what that one thing was, my friends thought I'd lost my mind.

"You get up every morning and do what with the rat?" they all asked.

"I mix a liquid steroid prescribed by the vet into strained peas baby food, and spoon feed it to Cagney," I sighed.

"You're nuts!" they all proclaimed.

I didn't tell them about my version of "rat physiotherapy." After he'd finished his baby food, I'd flip him over on his back and move his back legs as though he were pedaling a bicycle, to simulate the motion of walking. As the days and weeks passed, it was clear that the medication and the physio weren't working. Cagney would never be able to walk or sit up properly. We didn't know how old he was, but we resolved that we would make the remainder of his days happy ones.

He turned out to be a clever little fellow. In fact, on occasion he even managed to outsmart me. I found small stashes of his favorite foods hidden in the corners of his cage. He watched me replace them into his food dish a few times. Then one day, I caught him trying to push his food dish on top of the least favorite foods he had thrown to the floor. It reminded me of the way small children hide carrots and peas under their plates, thinking you won't notice.

Since his hind legs weren't strong enough, he couldn't sit up properly, which made self-grooming difficult. I would regularly take him out of his cage, flip him onto his back and scratch his head, neck and belly. He would close his eyes and lean back in pure bliss, loving every moment. Then, as if to return the favor, he would grab my fingers with both paws and lick them clean.

Every morning, he would shuffle out and, using his front paws, climb up a few bars of his cage to greet me. I would open the door and he would carefully climb out into my hands. I would cuddle him against my neck, between my shoulder and ear until he'd start to brux, the noise growing louder all the time.

When it was time for me to get down to the serious business of writing, he would curl up next to my laptop and either nap or snuffle about my desk. Occasionally, when he wanted attention, he would drop down into my lap and tug at my sweater until I took a break to give him a cuddle. Through many rough drafts, page after page, he was my constant companion.

But as I neared the end of my thesis, I knew that Cagney was nearing his end, too. He was slowing down, sleeping more and more. As I watched my loyal companion sleeping peacefully one afternoon, I thought, "If he can tough this out with me, then I can tough this out for him." Steadily I worked on, with Cagney by my side.

One morning, with only the last page of my thesis to go, I held Cagney in my hands and felt his heart beat for the last time.

As I looked at his tiny, furry body, I wondered how such a very small package could contain so much life, love and loyalty. If he was bothered by the lack of movement in his hind legs, I never knew. He would brux almost from the moment I picked him up until I put him down in his cage again. As the months passed, I was left to wonder how it was possible that something so small could leave such a large gap in someone's life as his passing had left in mine.

Shortly after I finished my thesis, my husband and I moved into our first home. There, I was able to bury Cagney in the yard near my office window, where I take comfort in the fact that he is still near me as I work.

We've gone on to adopt other pet rats that were in need of loving homes. While they may be the type of animal most people try to keep out of their homes, we have welcomed them into ours. Each is a precious little life with its own personality, but none has ever come close to matching our Cagney.

That's why, if you take my thesis down from the library shelf and turn to the acknowledgements page, you will find a single sentence at the very end, comprehensible only to those who know his story: "To Cagney—a most remarkable muse!"

Cagney, of the bright and shining eyes.

About the Author

 Though she has always loved animals, no one could have been more surprised than Crystal Parsons when she fell in love with a disabled rat named Cagney. Just how life-altering an experience this was is obvious, considering that Crystal has gone on to adopt or rescue many other rats, including her current companions, Scoops and Mr. Harry Hershey Bigglesworth. Crystal is currently an independent curator of Canadian art, a researcher and a writer. She holds a Masters degree in Canadian art history from Carleton University, and a Bachelor of Commerce degree from Memorial University of Newfoundland. She volunteers for the Heron Emergency Food Centre, a food bank in Ottawa, Ontario, Canada, her hometown. *Almost Perfect* marks Crystal's first foray into publication.

Pink Ears, Red Tape: Fritz
Roberta Beach Jacobson

2003

The little guy showed up at the kitchen door of our farmhouse and didn't hesitate for a second when I offered him a meaty meal along with our thirteen house cats. The pure white kitty, about a year old, took a quick look around our place and decided it would be suitable to his needs.

After eating his fill of chicken, he made his way around and headed up to our bed. As boldly as that.

My husband and I named him Fritz. My feather pillow became his favorite spot, and rarely was there a night when he didn't share it with me.

2004

Everyone, young and old, took to Fritz. Always cooperative and easygoing, he developed into a gentleman cat. Fritz never asked for special favors. He wasn't hard to please. Despite finding himself living in a multi-cat household, he wasn't one to pick fights or the type to make enemies.

We guessed he'd probably had a home at some point in his life, because he understood what toys meant. He enjoyed batting around ping-pong balls or wads of paper. The catnip mouse was another favorite.

In summer we noticed the tips of his ears sunburned easily, so we applied a powerful sunscreen. We'd asked at the pharmacy for a product that would be safe for babies and that meant it was good enough for our Fritz.

We may have plenty of sun where we live, but one thing the Greek island where we live lacks is a resident vet. Twice a year, volunteer vets arrive from Germany to spay/neuter. Fritz was on the list, along with a half-dozen other strays we'd rescued about the same time. Of the twenty, four-footed members of our household, nobody but Fritz had petal pink ears.

Our house resembled an animal shelter. Cats and kittens of every sort, along with our pair of pooches, napped or slept in baskets or boxes all over our living room floor. Some preferred the easy chairs. Fritz was adamant about claiming my feather pillow and stuck to that routine.

2005

As soon as the summer sun intensified, Fritz's ears lost fur. They remained shocking pink for four months. White cats are not native to arid Greece and white cats are more prone to sunburn, the volunteer veterinarian had explained to me. They have a higher incidence of developing skin cancer—particularly around the ears. Despite his shocking pink ears, Fritz remained a handsome lad.

Throughout the ages, strong male feline characters have been featured in poems and paintings, books and songs. Later cats featured prominently in movies and television (and more recently, in blogs). For his fifteen minutes of fame, Fritz became our poster boy for sun safety.

He captured the attention of tourists wandering through our tiny mountain village, cameras in hand. Many stopped to ask what was wrong with Fritz's ears. I was glad to recite the entire account over and over for them. Fritz knew he was the center of attention and rubbed against their legs while they tried to take his picture.

I warmed to the fact that tourists have pictures of Fritz included with their vacation memories of our island. Sometimes I've wondered if they got his name right when re-telling his tale to family and friends in their numerous European languages.

2006

No new crop of white hair appeared on Fritz's ear tips, a sign his condition had worsened. His ears started crusting. Open sores appeared, so we could no longer apply the sun cream (due to risk of skin poisoning).

It was clear to the volunteer vet, and to us, that Fritz's condition was in the danger zone. He never complained once about the discomfort. The walls of our house, splattered with blood from Fritz shaking his head, started to resemble a modern art studio. My husband and I admitted that what was best for Fritz would be to get away from the much-celebrated Greek sun and relocate to a dreary climate.

Cloudy days would be perfect for him, but where could he go?

We called friends in Holland and Germany, the wettest places we could think of. Could anyone take in another cat? Our Fritz needed help…and fast. I e-mailed a few of his photos to pet organizations, in case they had members who could help by offering a home.

Everyone was full. They'd adopted more pets, both cats and dogs, than planned. We understood well how fast such numbers can increase, as our personal cat count had since hit twenty-six (and our dog count three). We are not hoarders, but our island lacks an animal shelter and we seem to be where people turn when they have unwanted litters. We may cringe a little at the constant requests, but we don't say no.

2007

The volunteer vet examined Fritz and informed us his situation had turned critical. As she cleaned his outer ears, she told us his condition necessitated that he be moved to a cooler climate ASAP. There was no time to wait. He couldn't stand the harshness of another Greek summer, and it was fast approaching. We had to love Fritz enough to let him move away. We understood we had no other choice.

She made a few phone calls, starting with volunteer animal rescue organizations. Days later, she let us know two different families in Germany had expressed interest in adopting Fritz. She offered to take him along when she flew home the following week.

This was new, for one of our four-legged family members to move away from us. My husband and I figured we'd experienced just about everything when it came to rescuing and caring for kittens and cats. Since living on our far-flung island, we've patched up wounds, helped with births, nursed colds, bottle-fed orphan kittens, even removed fish hooks from the faces of harbor cats.

Soon it was mere days until we'd have to say goodbye to our mild-mannered feline with the hot pink ears. The volunteer vet suggested I include an article of clothing in Fritz's transport box as a personal touch, so a familiar scent would accompany him on his 1,200-mile journey.

It sounded like a great idea, so I dug through the laundry hampers. Amid the sheets and towels, I found nothing suitable. Then I remembered that my sports bra had rips on both sides, so I removed it and tied it in a knot, like a ball.

Fritz was micro-chipped in his neck and got issued his official European pet travel passport, fulfilling the red tape to cross any European border. The vet selected a sturdy travel box and found a plush towel to line it. I tossed in my bra.

Fritz had a one-way air ticket to Dusseldorf, Germany and I hoped his future would be full of rainy days. How ironic that the sun, which lures so many tourists to hang out on Greek beaches, was what caused harm to Fritz. During the long July and August days, we peak at twelve and a half hours of its hot rays.

It was a somber drive, delivering Fritz to the island's tiny airport. Fritz-the-gentleman-cat had been with us for more than four years. I was grateful he had the chance for a new life in a place full of clouds, but I sensed my pillow would feel half-empty without his presence.

I looked over at Fritz in his plastic airliner case and hoped the new sounds in Germany would be pleasing to his ears. He didn't know it yet, but the typical Greek sounds of braying donkeys and chirping cicadas he'd grown used to would represent his past. His new sounds might be voices in an apartment building, frequent rain showers, school children skipping down the sidewalk.

Change was in the air. Instead of living in a rural house with twenty-five other cats and three dogs as he had with us, Fritz's new home would be a suburban apartment with just two other cats.

Fritz was a cabin passenger and the direct charter flight went smoothly. The transfer to his new family was easy, the volunteer vet told me. In fact, they lived just a hop, skip and a jump from the vet clinic.

The new owner called the vet hours after Fritz had been dropped off.

"Is everything all right?" the veterinarian asked, worry creeping into her voice.

"Just a strange question," replied the caller. "Why in the world does Fritz have a bra?"

Fritz, showing signs of his losing battle with the searing Greek sun.

About the Author

Roberta Beach Jacobson is a full-time freelance writer who specializes in travel writing and stories about animals. Her wry wit causes her work to tend toward the humorous, even when writing about serious subjects. Roberta has shared that work in more than forty anthologies including *Chicken Soup*, *Cup of Comfort* (Adams Media), and *Chocolate for Women* (Simon & Schuster). Her work has been published on four continents, and she blogs regularly as "The Cat Lady" for the *Seattle Post Intelligencer's* website. Roberta lives on the beautiful Greek island of Karpathos, where she first met Fritz. The all-white cat with petal pink ears became an inspiration, the story she shares in *Almost Perfect*. Roberta is a regular contributor to several cat publications. She is a founding member of Animal Welfare Karpathos, where she volunteers regularly, and a Professional member of the Cat Writers' Association.